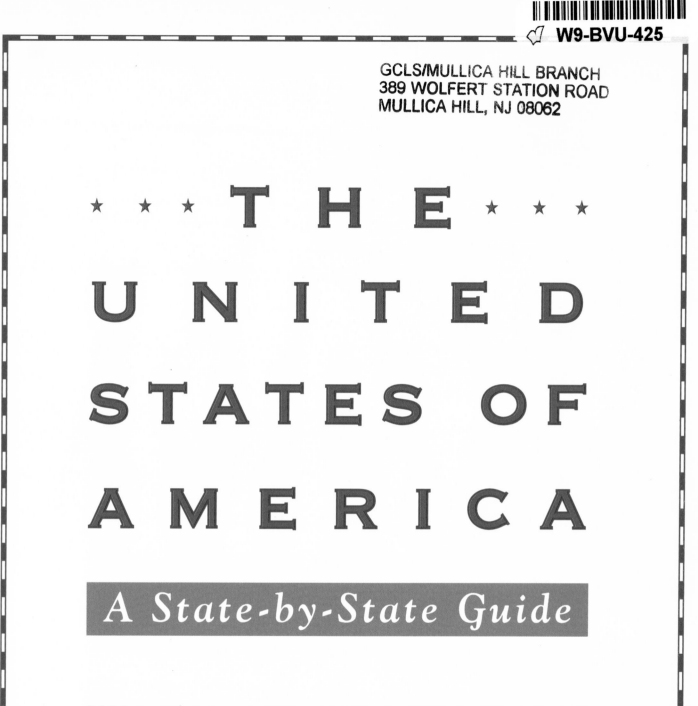

★ ★ ★ T H E ★ ★ ★ U N I T E D S T A T E S O F A M E R I C A

A State-by-State Guide

MILLIE MILLER AND CYNDI NELSON

★ ★ ★

SCHOLASTIC REFERENCE

Acknowledgments

Thank you, Ivan and Scott, our enduring husbands and critics.
Tell the kids—Scott, Jon, Tyler, Peter, Jeffrey, and Stina—that we'll be home for dinner.

Special thanks for valuable input to:

Audrey Benedict (Cloud Ridge Naturalists), Brad Easterson (American PIE—Public Information on the Environment), Nancy Laties Feresten (Senior Editor, Scholastic Inc.), Barbara French (Bat Conservation International), Steve Frye and Scott Severs (Boulder Wild Bird Center), Laurie Lanzen Harris (Editor of *Biography Today*, Omnigraphics, Inc.), Boris Kondratieff (Ft. Collins Entomology Department), Chris Pague (The Nature Conservancy), Gerry Roehm (The U.S. Fish and Wildlife Service), Nancy Sabato (Art Director, Scholastic Inc.), Judy Volc (Children's Literature Specialist, Boulder Public Library), Katherine Young and Fran Grzenda (Foothill Elementary Librarians, Boulder, CO), all the folks at Scholastic Inc. who made this project possible, and the many people throughout the U.S.A. who answered our endless questions.

Additional thanks to our support team:

Dr. John Carter (southern gentleman), Ginny Gardner (our Hawaiian connection), Bill and Lyn Gullette (Endaba, Pagosa Springs B&B), Marcy Lockhart (world traveler and teacher), Jake Lucas (resident Montana expert), Carl Mackey (Plant Ecologist, Rocky Mountain Arsenal National Wildlife Refuge), Marilyn Marinelli (educator extraordinaire), Walt and Velma Nelson (grandparents), and Ana Sanjuan (steadfast source of encouragement and nourishment).

Population statistics for the 50 states, Washington, D.C., and Puerto Rico are from the U.S. Census Bureau's Census 2000 data (www.census.gov).

★   ★   ★   ★

ISBN 0-439-27259-9

12 11 10 9 8 7 6 5 4 3 2   02 03 04 05

Printed in the U.S.A.   14

First trade paperback printing, August 2001

Book design by Nancy Sabato
Composition by BNGO Books/Kevin Callahan

Dedicated to the
Children of the World

"The survival of
the world depends
upon our sharing what
we have and
working together."

— Frank Fools Crow,
Teton Sioux

CANADA

The U.S.-Canadian Border is the longest undefended border in the world.

WASHINGTON

Missouri River

OREGON

NORTH DAKOTA

MONTANA

Cascade Mountains

IDAHO

WYOMING

SOUTH DAKOTA

Continental Divide

Rocky

NEBRASKA

Sierra Nevada Mountains

Pacific Ocean

NEVADA

UTAH

Mountains

COLORADO

KANSAS

CALIFORNIA

Colorado River

Death Valley is the lowest spot in the nation, at 282 feet below sea level.

ARIZONA

NEW MEXICO

National bird: Bald eagle

The northernmost point in the U.S.A. is Point Barrow, AK.

MEXICO

Rio Grande

TEXAS

Each year, it rains about 460 inches on the wettest place in the world, Mt. Waialeale, Kauai.

ALASKA

HAWAII

Cape Wrangel, AK, is the westernmost point in the U.S.A.

Denali is the highest mountain in North America. It is 20,320 feet.

Ka Lae, HI, is the southernmost point in the U.S.A.

The United States of America was founded July 4, 1776. • Population: 281,421,906 • Area: 3,675,031 square miles

Lake Superior is the largest freshwater lake in the world.

The St. Lawrence Seaway is the longest canal in the world. It is about 450 miles long.

The easternmost point in the U.S.A. is West Quoddy Head, ME.

CANADA

MINNESOTA

Lake Superior

MICHIGAN

WISCONSIN

Lake Huron

St. Lawrence River

MAINE

Lake Michigan

MICHIGAN

Lake Ontario

VERMONT

NEW HAMPSHIRE

NEW YORK

MASSACHUSETTS

IOWA

Lake Erie

RHODE ISLAND

CONNECTICUT

ILLINOIS

INDIANA

OHIO

PENNSYLVANIA

NEW JERSEY

Missouri River

Mississippi River

Ohio River

DELAWARE

WEST VIRGINIA

Appalachian Mountains

MARYLAND

WASHINGTON, D.C.

KENTUCKY

VIRGINIA

MISSOURI

MISSOURI

TENNESSEE

NORTH CAROLINA

OKLAHOMA

ARKANSAS

SOUTH CAROLINA

Extinct: Carolina parakeet. Over 250 U.S. plants and animals have disappeared since 1980.

MISSISSIPPI

ALABAMA

GEORGIA

Atlantic Ocean

LOUISIANA

FLORIDA

The Mississippi River is 2,348 miles long. It is the longest river in North America.

Gulf of Mexico

National flower: Rose

Puerto Rico is a U.S. commonwealth and located about 1,000 miles southeast of Miami.

PUERTO RICO

THE UNITED STATES OF AMERICA

People lived in Russell Cave for 8,000 years, from 6500 B.C. to A.D. 1500. We know because they left bones and tools behind.

State bird: Yellow-shafted flicker

This woodpecker is also called "yellow-hammer."

State flower: Camellia

Alabama Space and Rocket Center is where scientists developed the first rocket to put people on the moon.

The Mississippian mound builders built temple mounds for ceremonies. One in Moundville is still standing after 800 years.

George Washington Carver (1864–1943), an agricultural scientist at Tuskegee University, developed hundreds of uses for peanuts and sweet potatoes in the early 1900s.

In 1955, African-Americans had to ride in the back of buses and give up a seat if a white person was standing. Rosa Parks (b. 1913 in Tuskegee) refused to give up her seat on a Montgomery bus. The bus boycott that followed was the beginning of the end of segregation.

State insect: The monarch butterfly flies to Mexico for the winter.

Endangered species: Red Hills salamander needs steep hardwood-forest slopes to burrow in.

State tree: Southern pine. Alabama is famous for its pine forests. The trees are made into paper products, the state's biggest industry.

TENNESSEE
MISSISSIPPI
GEORGIA
FLORIDA
Tennessee River
Huntsville
Appalachian Mountains
Black Sipsey River
Birmingham
Warrior River
Moundville
Cahaba River
Coosa River
Cheaha Mt. 2,407 ft.
Tallapoosa River
Lake Martin
Tuskegee
Selma
MONTGOMERY
Chattahoochee River
Red Hills
Tombigbee River
Alabama River
Mobile River
Mobile Bay
Gulf of Mexico

Alabama
Heart of Dixie

22nd state • Statehood: December 14, 1819 • Population: 4,447,100 • Area: 52,423 square miles

State bird: The willow ptarmigan is white in the winter and brown in the summer.

The aurora borealis is the northern-light display that brightens the 24-hour winter nights. In the summer, Alaska is the land of the midnight sun.

There are no roads in much of Alaska: 1 in 68 people are pilots.

Polar bears are well-adapted to the arctic cold.

Point Barrow: Northernmost point in U.S.A.

Prudhoe Bay

Arctic Ocean

Brooks Range

State tree: Sitka spruce

Bering Strait

Kotzebue

Arctic Circle

Fort Yukon

Dogsled races over snow are popular. The Iditarod race from Anchorage to Nome is world famous.

Nome

Yukon River

Circle

Fairbanks

Denali: Highest peak in N.A. 20,320 ft.

CANADA

Cedar totem poles of NW coastal tribes are sometimes 80 feet tall.

Alaska is almost 1/5 as large as the rest of the U.S.A.

Bethel

Alaska Range

Wrangel St. Elias Mts.

Anchorage

Valdez

JUNEAU

Horned puffins fish off the Aleutian Islands.

Seward

Cook Inlet

Gulf of Alaska

Sitka

Ketchikan

Kodiak Island is home to the largest brown bears on earth.

Juneau is the only state capital that can't be reached by road.

Aleutian Islands

Pacific Ocean

State flower: Forget-me-not

Cape Wrangle: Westernmost point in the U.S.A.

Endangered species: Humpback whales are often seen in summer off Alaska's coast, where cold arctic waters provide plenty of rich plankton to eat.

Alaska
Last Frontier

49th state • Statehood: January 3, 1959 • Population: 626,932 • Area: 656,424 square miles

Endangered species: Sandborn's lesser longnosed bat is a vital part of the nighttime pollination of the saguaro cactus.

The Grand Canyon is a scenic 277-mile-long gorge, one mile deep in some places.

UTAH   COLORADO

Colorado   Plateau

Four Corners

NEVADA

Colorado River

Canyon de Chelly was home to prehistoric Pueblo Indians.

State tree: Paloverde

Lake Mead

Painted Desert

Little Colorado River

Humphrey's Peak 12,633 ft.

Petrified Forest

NEW MEXICO

Flagstaff

Hoover Dam regulates the flow of the Colorado River. Its huge generators use the energy of the moving water to make electricity.

CALIFORNIA

Colorado River

Magollon Rim

State flower: Blossoms of the saguaro cactus, the largest cactus in the U.S.A., bloom at night in the Sonoran Desert.

PHOENIX • Scottsdale

• Tempe

Salt River

Gila River

Gila River

Yuma

Sonoran Desert

Santa Cruz River

Tucson •

Kitt Peak National Observatory

• Tombstone

Skeleton ▲ Canyon

MEXICO

The Tucson area is called the Astronomy Capital of the world because of good star viewing away from city lights and pollution.

Tombstone was a boomtown of the Old West known for gunfights and a cemetery called Boot Hill.

RIP

Geronimo (1829-1909) was a legendary Apache leader. In 1886, his tribe was one of the last to surrender to U.S. troops (in Skeleton Canyon).

State bird: The cactus wren builds a football-shaped nest in several kinds of cactus.

Arizona
Grand Canyon State

48th state • Statehood: February 14, 1912 • Population: 5,130,632 • Area: 114,006 square miles

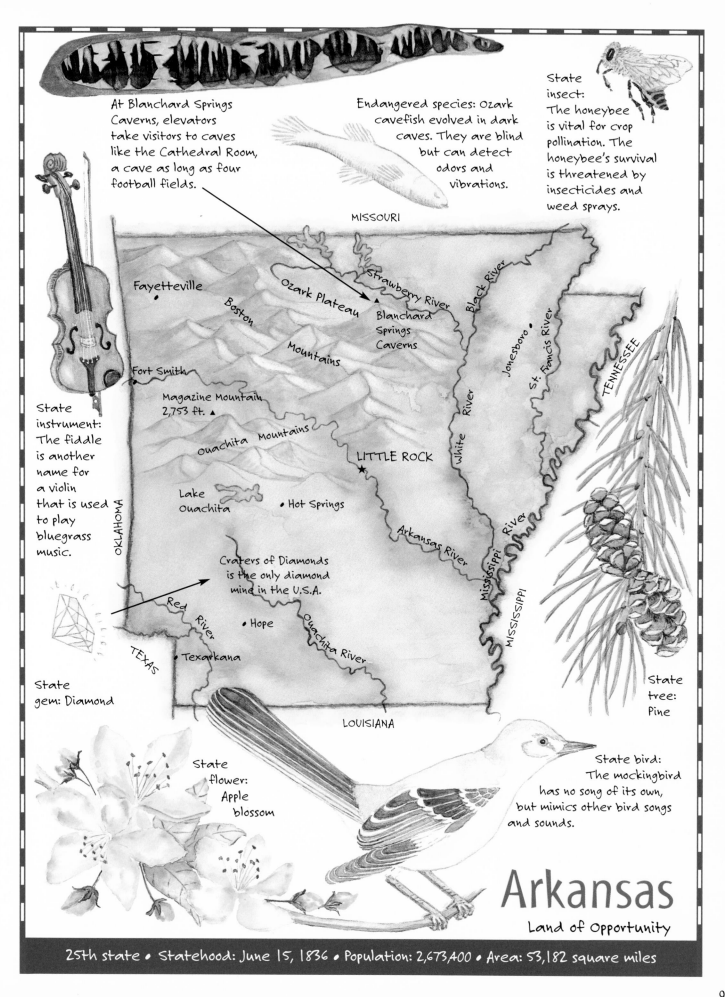

At Blanchard Springs Caverns, elevators take visitors to caves like the Cathedral Room, a cave as long as four football fields.

Endangered species: Ozark cavefish evolved in dark caves. They are blind but can detect odors and vibrations.

State insect: The honeybee is vital for crop pollination. The honeybee's survival is threatened by insecticides and weed sprays.

State instrument: The fiddle is another name for a violin that is used to play bluegrass music.

State gem: Diamond

Craters of Diamonds is the only diamond mine in the U.S.A.

MISSOURI

Fayetteville

Ozark Plateau

Strawberry River

Black River

Blanchard Springs Caverns

Boston

Mountains

Jonesboro

St. Francis River

TENNESSEE

Fort Smith

Magazine Mountain 2,753 ft. ▲

Ouachita Mountains

LITTLE ROCK

White River

Lake Ouachita

Hot Springs

Arkansas River

Mississippi River

OKLAHOMA

Red River

Hope

Ouachita River

Mississippi

TEXAS

Texarkana

LOUISIANA

State tree: Pine

State flower: Apple blossom

State bird: The mockingbird has no song of its own, but mimics other bird songs and sounds.

Arkansas

Land of Opportunity

25th state • Statehood: June 15, 1836 • Population: 2,673,400 • Area: 53,182 square miles

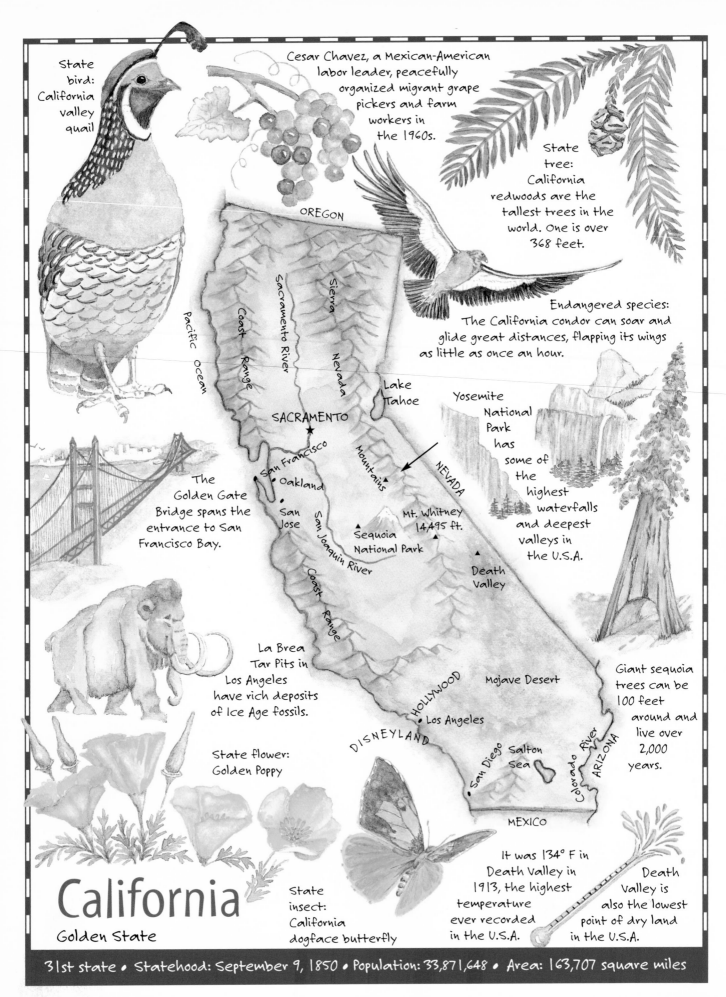

State bird: California valley quail

Cesar Chavez, a Mexican-American labor leader, peacefully organized migrant grape pickers and farm workers in the 1960s.

State tree: California redwoods are the tallest trees in the world. One is over 368 feet.

Endangered species: The California condor can soar and glide great distances, flapping its wings as little as once an hour.

Yosemite National Park has some of the highest waterfalls and deepest valleys in the U.S.A.

The Golden Gate Bridge spans the entrance to San Francisco Bay.

La Brea Tar Pits in Los Angeles have rich deposits of Ice Age fossils.

State flower: Golden Poppy

Giant sequoia trees can be 100 feet around and live over 2,000 years.

It was 134° F in Death Valley in 1913, the highest temperature ever recorded in the U.S.A.

Death Valley is also the lowest point of dry land in the U.S.A.

State insect: California dogface butterfly

California

Golden State

Map labels: OREGON · Pacific Ocean · Coast Range · Sacramento River · Sierra Nevada · SACRAMENTO · Lake Tahoe · San Francisco · Oakland · San Jose · San Joaquin River · Mountains · NEVADA · Mt. Whitney 14,495 ft. · Sequoia National Park · Death Valley · Coast Range · HOLLYWOOD · Mojave Desert · Los Angeles · DISNEYLAND · San Diego · Salton Sea · Colorado River · ARIZONA · MEXICO

31st state • Statehood: September 9, 1850 • Population: 33,871,648 • Area: 163,707 square miles

State tree: Blue spruce

The Colorado Mountains have some of the best skiing in the world.

Gold and silver are mined in the Rocky Mountains. In 1894, the largest silver nugget (1,840 pounds) in North America was unearthed in Aspen.

State bird: The lark bunting nests in the dry sagebrush plains and prairies of Colorado.

Large dinosaur fossil deposits are found here.

WYOMING

NEBRASKA

Dinosaur National Monument

The Continental Divide stretches the length of the Colorado Rockies; water runs off east to the Atlantic Ocean and west to the Pacific Ocean.

Continental Divide

ROCKY MOUNTAINS

Fort Collins

Boulder

Greeley

South Platte River

Colorado River

Vail

Denver, the Mile High City, is 5,280 feet above sea level.

DENVER

Aspen

Mt. Elbert 14,433 ft.

Colorado Springs

Pikes Peak

The cry of the 1858 gold rush was "Pikes Peak or Bust."

Gunnison River

Pueblo

Arkansas River

KANSAS

Dolores River

At Four Corners you can touch four states at once.

Rio Grande River

San Juan River

Endangered species: The greenback cutthroat trout is threatened by disease and inbreeding.

UTAH

Mesa Verde

COLORADO

NEW MEXICO

ARIZONA

OKLAHOMA

Ancient Anasazi cliff dwellings

State insect: Colorado hairstreak

State flower: Rocky Mountain columbine

Colorado

Centennial State

38th state • Statehood: August 1, 1876 • Population: 4,301,261 • Area: 104,100 square miles

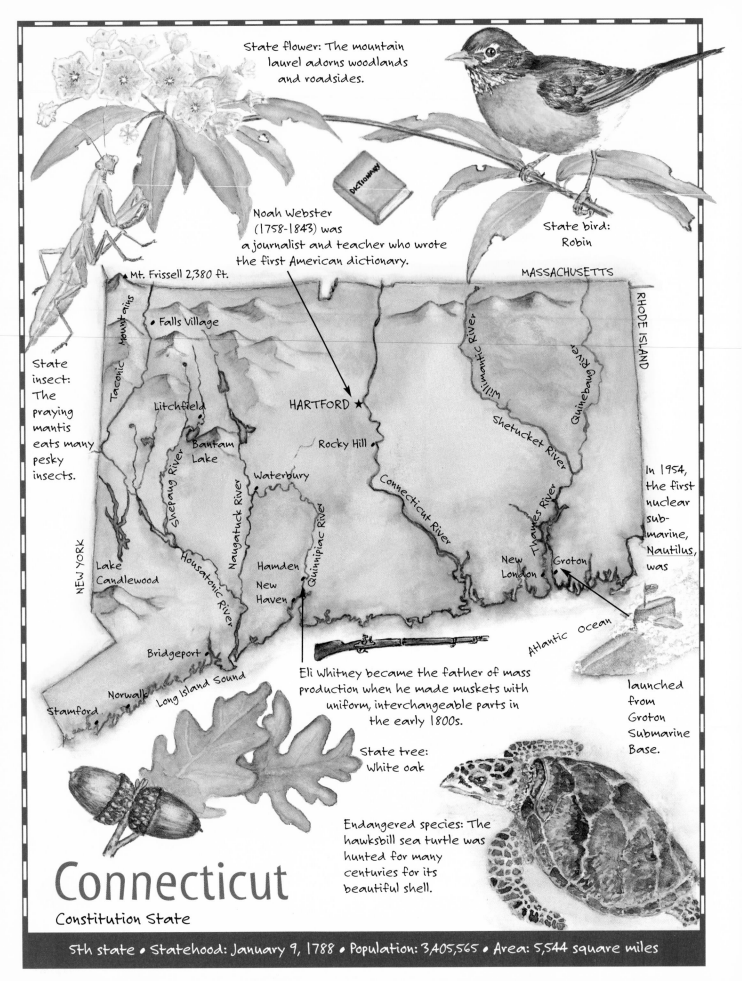

State flower: The mountain laurel adorns woodlands and roadsides.

State bird: Robin

Noah Webster (1758-1843) was a journalist and teacher who wrote the first American dictionary.

DICTIONARY

MASSACHUSETTS

RHODE ISLAND

Mt. Frissell 2,380 ft.

State insect: The praying mantis eats many pesky insects.

Taconic Mountains

• Falls Village

Willimantic River

Quinebaug River

Litchfield

HARTFORD ★

Shetucket River

Bantam Lake

Rocky Hill •

Shepaug River

Waterbury

Connecticut River

Naugatuck River

Quinnipiac River

Thames River

In 1954, the first nuclear sub-marine, Nautilus, was

NEW YORK

Lake Candlewood

Housatonic River

Hamden

New Haven

New London

Groton

Bridgeport •

Eli Whitney became the father of mass production when he made muskets with uniform, interchangeable parts in the early 1800s.

Atlantic Ocean

launched from Groton Submarine Base.

Norwalk •

Long Island Sound

Stamford •

State tree: White oak

Endangered species: The hawksbill sea turtle was hunted for many centuries for its beautiful shell.

Connecticut

Constitution State

5th state • Statehood: January 9, 1788 • Population: 3,405,565 • Area: 5,544 square miles

State flower: Peach blossom

Nylon was invented in 1938 in Wilmington, making Delaware a leader in the chemical industry.

Most of the state was once covered by the ocean. Many extinct fossilized sea creatures have been found there.

State bird: Blue hen chicken

Delaware's leading cash farm product is broiler chickens. Hundreds of millions of them are raised in Sussex County yearly.

State insect: Ladybug

PENNSYLVANIA

Wilmington
Newark
Christina River
Delaware River
New Castle
Delaware City
Chesapeake & Delaware Canal
Middletown
Smyrna River
Smyrna
Delaware Bay
DOVER ★
St. Jones River
Harrington
Mispillion River
Milford
Atlantic Ocean
Broadkill River
Gravelly Brook
Lewes
Rehoboth Bay
Seaford
Nanticoke River
Georgetown
Sussex County
Laurel
Pocomoke River
Indian River Bay
Cypress Swamp
Selbyville
Fenwick Island
MARYLAND

About 1638, near the mouth of the Delaware River, Swedish and Finnish settlers built the first log cabins in North America.

Endangered species: The Delmarva Peninsula fox squirrel needs mature forests along streams, bays, and salt marshes.

State tree: American holly has separate male and female trees.

The northernmost cypress swamp in the U.S.A. is an ancient bald-cypress and cedar forest.

Delaware
First State

1st state • Statehood: December 7, 1787 • Population: 783,600 • Area: 2,489 square miles

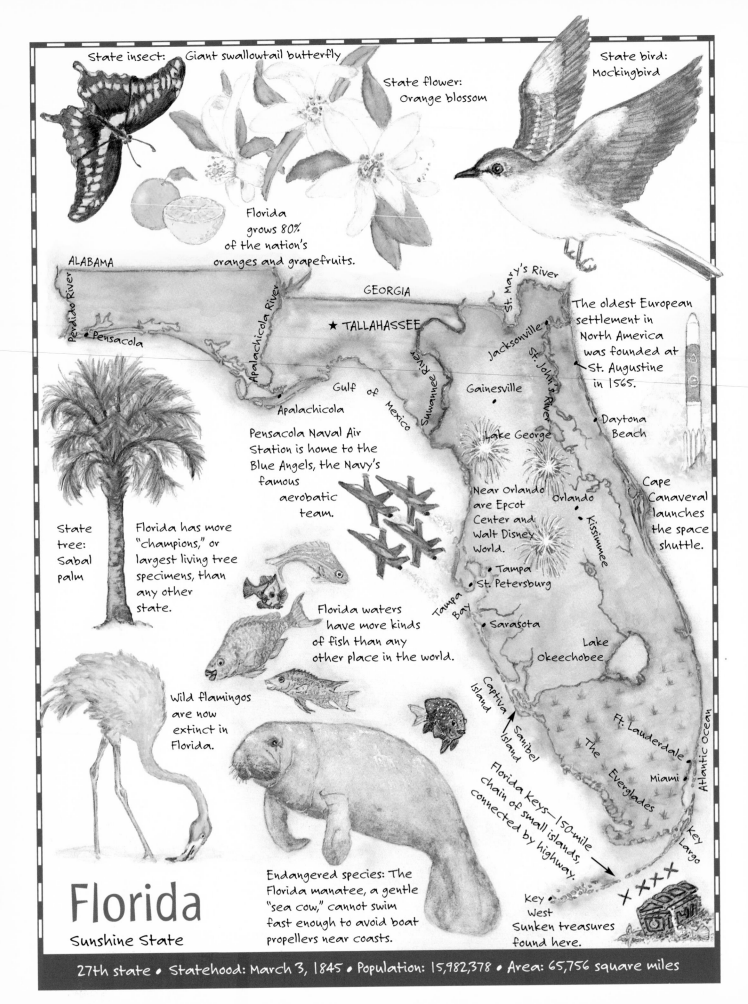

State insect: Giant swallowtail butterfly

State flower: Orange blossom

State bird: Mockingbird

Florida grows 80% of the nation's oranges and grapefruits.

ALABAMA

GEORGIA

Perdido River

Pensacola

Apalachicola River

★ TALLAHASSEE

St. Mary's River

Jacksonville

St. John's River

The oldest European settlement in North America was founded at St. Augustine in 1565.

Gulf of Mexico

Suwannee River

Apalachicola

Gainesville

Lake George

Daytona Beach

Pensacola Naval Air Station is home to the Blue Angels, the Navy's famous aerobatic team.

Near Orlando are Epcot Center and Walt Disney World.

Orlando

Kissimmee

Cape Canaveral launches the space shuttle.

State tree: Sabal palm

Florida has more "champions," or largest living tree specimens, than any other state.

Florida waters have more kinds of fish than any other place in the world.

Tampa

St. Petersburg

Tampa Bay

Sarasota

Lake Okeechobee

Wild flamingos are now extinct in Florida.

Captiva Island

Sanibel Island

Ft. Lauderdale

The Everglades

Miami

Atlantic Ocean

Florida Keys—150-mile chain of small islands, connected by highway.

Key Largo

Key West

Sunken treasures found here.

Endangered species: The Florida manatee, a gentle "sea cow," cannot swim fast enough to avoid boat propellers near coasts.

Florida

Sunshine State

27th state • Statehood: March 3, 1845 • Population: 15,982,378 • Area: 65,756 square miles

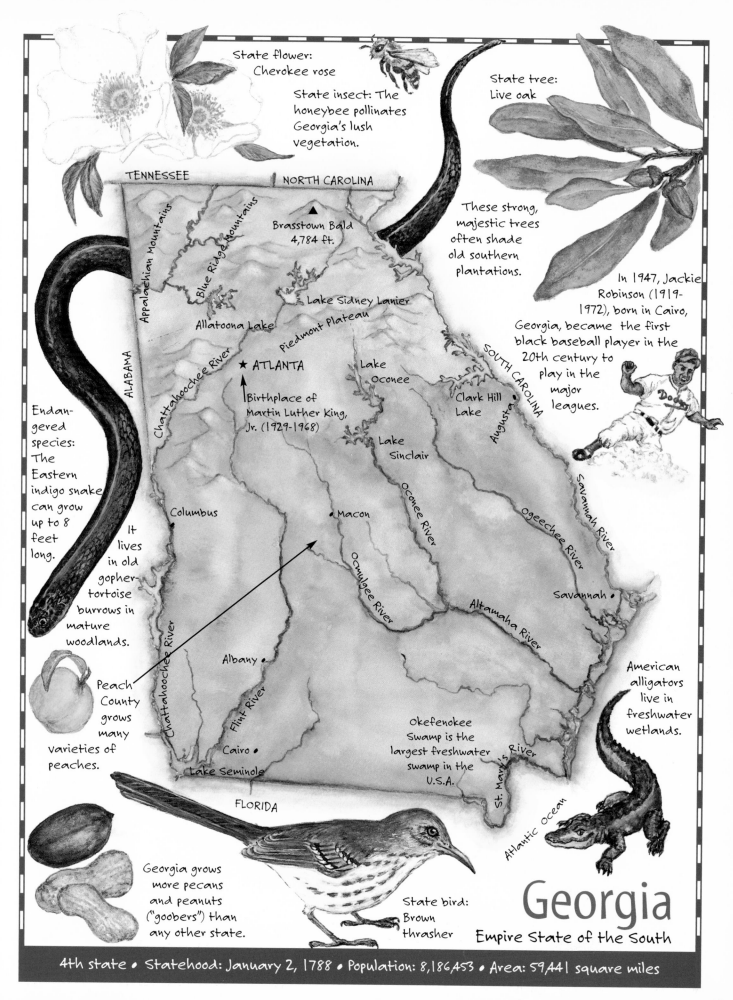

State flower:
Cherokee rose

State insect: The honeybee pollinates Georgia's lush vegetation.

State tree: Live oak

These strong, majestic trees often shade old southern plantations.

In 1947, Jackie Robinson (1919-1972), born in Cairo, Georgia, became the first black baseball player in the 20th century to play in the major leagues.

Endangered species: The Eastern indigo snake can grow up to 8 feet long. It lives in old gopher-tortoise burrows in mature woodlands.

Peach County grows many varieties of peaches.

American alligators live in freshwater wetlands.

Georgia grows more pecans and peanuts ("goobers") than any other state.

State bird: Brown thrasher

TENNESSEE

NORTH CAROLINA

Brasstown Bald 4,784 ft.

Appalachian Mountains

Blue Ridge Mountains

Lake Sidney Lanier

Allatoona Lake

Piedmont Plateau

ALABAMA

Chattahoochee River

★ ATLANTA

Birthplace of Martin Luther King, Jr. (1929-1968)

Lake Oconee

SOUTH CAROLINA

Clark Hill Lake

Augusta

Lake Sinclair

Oconee River

Columbus

Macon

Ogeechee River

Savannah River

Savannah

Altamaha River

Ocmulgee River

Albany

Flint River

Chattahoochee River

Cairo

Lake Seminole

FLORIDA

Okefenokee Swamp is the largest freshwater swamp in the U.S.A.

St. Mary's River

Atlantic Ocean

Georgia
Empire State of the South

4th state • Statehood: January 2, 1788 • Population: 8,186,453 • Area: 59,441 square miles

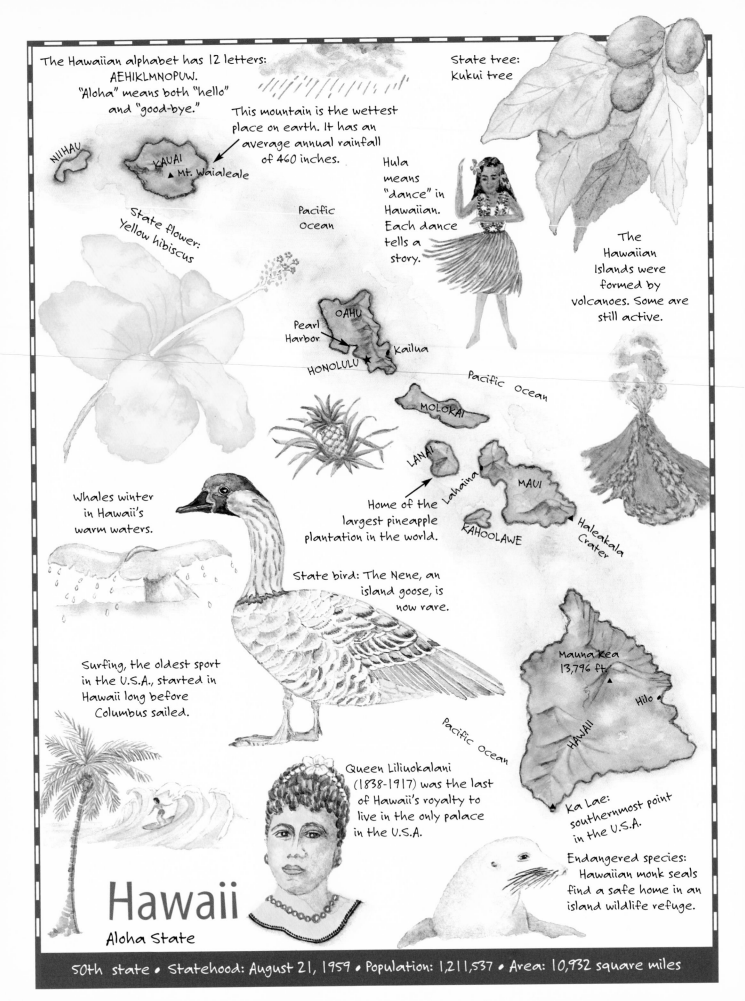

The Hawaiian alphabet has 12 letters: AEHIKLMNOPUW. "Aloha" means both "hello" and "good-bye."

State tree: kukui tree

This mountain is the wettest place on earth. It has an average annual rainfall of 460 inches.

NIIHAU

KAUAI ▲ Mt. Waialeale

Hula means "dance" in Hawaiian. Each dance tells a story.

Pacific Ocean

State flower: Yellow hibiscus

The Hawaiian Islands were formed by volcanoes. Some are still active.

OAHU
Pearl Harbor
Kailua
HONOLULU

Pacific Ocean

MOLOKAI

LANAI
Lahaina
MAUI
KAHOOLAWE
Haleakala Crater

Home of the largest pineapple plantation in the world.

Whales winter in Hawaii's warm waters.

State bird: The Nene, an island goose, is now rare.

Surfing, the oldest sport in the U.S.A., started in Hawaii long before Columbus sailed.

Mauna Kea 13,796 ft. ▲
Hilo •
HAWAII

Pacific Ocean

Queen Liliuokalani (1838-1917) was the last of Hawaii's royalty to live in the only palace in the U.S.A.

Ka Lae: southernmost point in the U.S.A.

Endangered species: Hawaiian monk seals find a safe home in an island wildlife refuge.

Hawaii
Aloha State

50th state • Statehood: August 21, 1959 • Population: 1,211,537 • Area: 10,932 square miles

16

State insect: Monarch butterfly

State bird: Mountain bluebird

Sacagawea, born in Idaho, was a teenage Shoshone who helped guide the Lewis and Clark Expedition from North Dakota to the Pacific Ocean. She carried her baby with her.

Endangered species: Woodland caribou live in coniferous forests near Canada.

State Tree: Western white pine

CANADA

MONTANA

WASHINGTON

Lake Pend Oreille

• Coeur d'Alene

• Lewiston

ROCKY MOUNTAINS

Salmon River

The Salmon River was named "The River of No Return" for its ferocious rapids.

At Sun Valley ski resort, the world's first ski lift began operation in 1935.

Borah Peak 12,662 ft. ▲

Continental Divide

Sun Valley •

★ BOISE

Idaho Falls

• Pocatello

WYOMING

State flower: Syringa

OREGON

Snake River

• Twin Falls

American Falls

The Crystal Ice Cave displays formations of ice and stone.

Balanced Rock is 40 feet high and rests on a small block of stone.

NEVADA   UTAH

More potatoes are grown in the fertile Snake River valley than in any other place in the U.S.A.

Idaho
Gem State

43rd state • Statehood: July 3, 1890 • Population: 1,293,953 • Area: 83,574 square miles

State insect: Monarch butterfly

In 1893, the original Ferris wheel was built for the World's Columbian Exposition. 2,160 people could ride at one time.

WISCONSIN

Rockford

Lake Michigan

O'Hare Airport is the world's busiest; a plane lands or takes off every 30 seconds.

Chicago

Joliet

Endangered species: Hine's emerald dragonfly is found in bogs and undisturbed streams.

IOWA

Rock River

Mississippi River

The "El," an elevated train that circles Chicago's downtown "Loop," started running in November 1897.

Abraham Lincoln (1809-1865) was an honest Illinois lawyer before becoming our 16th President.

Illinois River

Peoria

Champaign

INDIANA

State bird: Cardinal

Quincy

New Salem

SPRINGFIELD

Sangamon River

Decatur

Kaskaskia River

Lake Shelbyville

Monk's Mound, built by ancient Mississippian peoples, is the largest Indian mound in North America. Its base is bigger than that of the great pyramid of Egypt.

Missouri River

Mississippi River

East St. Louis

Cahokia

Carlyle Lake

Wabash River

Male

MISSOURI

Big Muddy River

Rend Lake

Cave in Rock X

KENTUCKY

State flower: Violet

Ohio River

X marks the spot of an old pirate hideout.

State tree: White oaks grow to be over 100 feet tall.

Illinois
Land of Lincoln

21st state • Statehood: December 3, 1818 • Population: 12,419,293 • Area: 57,918 square miles

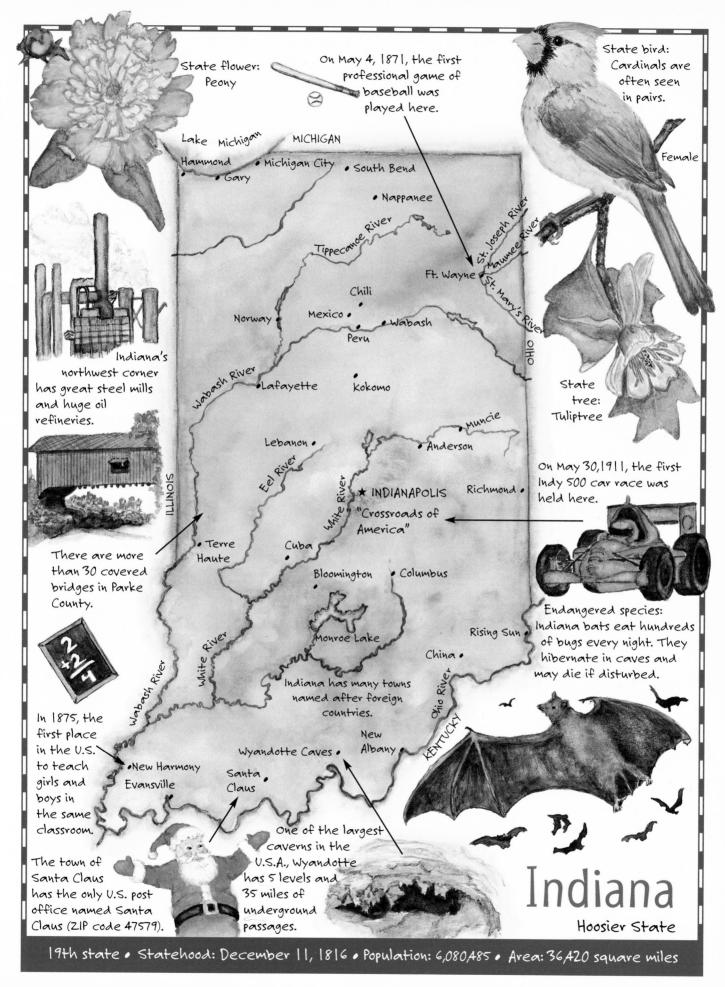

State flower: Peony

On May 4, 1871, the first professional game of baseball was played here.

State bird: Cardinals are often seen in pairs.

Female

Lake Michigan

MICHIGAN

Hammond
Gary
Michigan City
South Bend
Nappanee

Tippecanoe River

St. Joseph River
Maumee River
Ft. Wayne
St. Mary's River
OHIO

Chili
Norway
Mexico
Wabash
Peru

State tree: Tuliptree

Indiana's northwest corner has great steel mills and huge oil refineries.

Wabash River

Lafayette
Kokomo

Muncie

Lebanon
Anderson

Eel River

White River

★ INDIANAPOLIS
"Crossroads of America"

Richmond

On May 30, 1911, the first Indy 500 car race was held here.

ILLINOIS

There are more than 30 covered bridges in Parke County.

Terre Haute
Cuba

Bloomington
Columbus

Monroe Lake

Rising Sun

China

Endangered species: Indiana bats eat hundreds of bugs every night. They hibernate in caves and may die if disturbed.

Wabash River

White River

Indiana has many towns named after foreign countries.

Ohio River

In 1875, the first place in the U.S. to teach girls and boys in the same classroom.

New Harmony
Evansville

Santa Claus

Wyandotte Caves

New Albany

KENTUCKY

The town of Santa Claus has the only U.S. post office named Santa Claus (ZIP code 47579).

One of the largest caverns in the U.S.A., Wyandotte has 5 levels and 35 miles of underground passages.

Indiana
Hoosier State

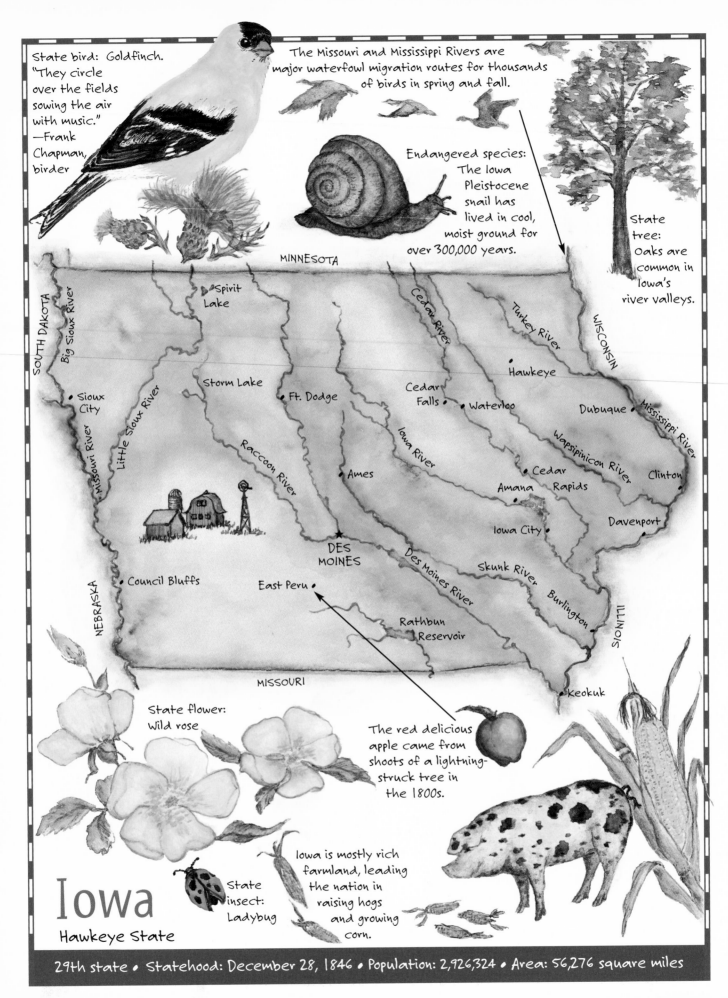

State bird: Goldfinch. "They circle over the fields sowing the air with music." —Frank Chapman, birder

The Missouri and Mississippi Rivers are major waterfowl migration routes for thousands of birds in spring and fall.

Endangered species: The Iowa Pleistocene snail has lived in cool, moist ground for over 300,000 years.

State tree: Oaks are common in Iowa's river valleys.

MINNESOTA

SOUTH DAKOTA

Big Sioux River

Spirit Lake

Cedar River

Turkey River

WISCONSIN

Storm Lake

Ft. Dodge

Hawkeye

Sioux City

Little Sioux River

Cedar Falls

Waterloo

Dubuque

Mississippi River

Missouri River

Raccoon River

Iowa River

Wapsipinicon River

Clinton

Ames

Cedar Rapids

Amana

Davenport

Iowa City

DES MOINES

Des Moines River

Skunk River

Council Bluffs

East Peru

Burlington

NEBRASKA

Rathbun Reservoir

ILLINOIS

MISSOURI

Keokuk

State flower: Wild rose

The red delicious apple came from shoots of a lightning-struck tree in the 1800s.

State insect: Ladybug

Iowa is mostly rich farmland, leading the nation in raising hogs and growing corn.

Iowa

Hawkeye State

29th state • Statehood: December 28, 1846 • Population: 2,926,324 • Area: 56,276 square miles

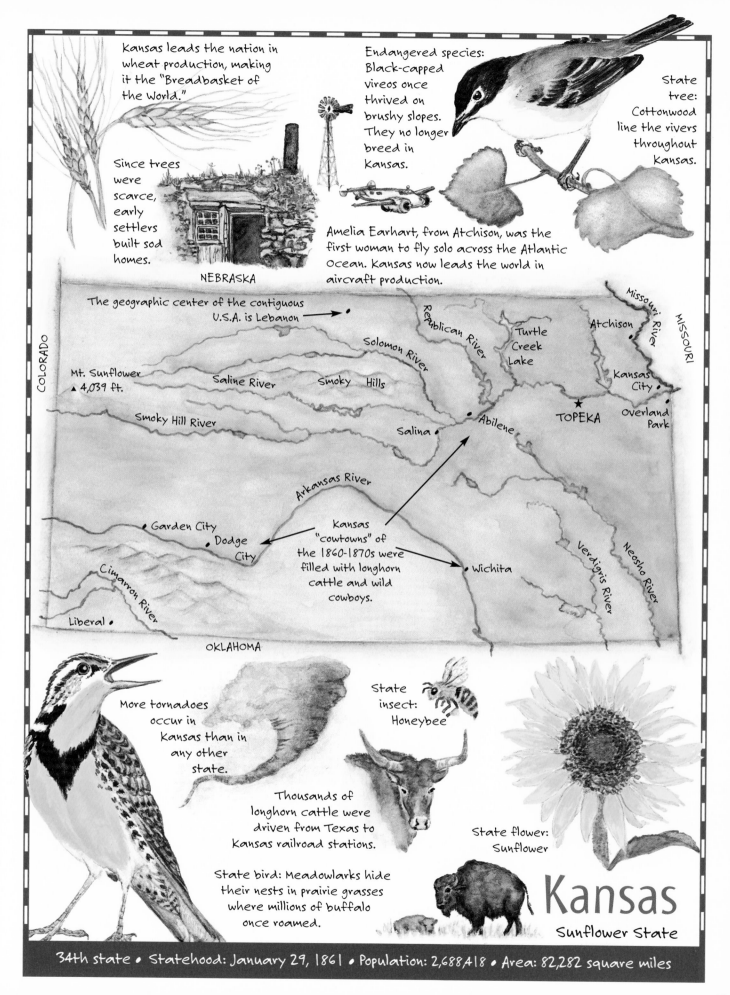

Kansas leads the nation in wheat production, making it the "Breadbasket of the World."

Since trees were scarce, early settlers built sod homes.

Endangered species: Black-capped vireos once thrived on brushy slopes. They no longer breed in Kansas.

State tree: Cottonwood line the rivers throughout Kansas.

Amelia Earhart, from Atchison, was the first woman to fly solo across the Atlantic Ocean. Kansas now leads the world in aircraft production.

NEBRASKA

The geographic center of the contiguous U.S.A. is Lebanon

Republican River
Solomon River
Turtle Creek Lake
Missouri River
Atchison
MISSOURI
Mt. Sunflower ▲ 4,039 ft.
Saline River
Smoky Hills
Kansas City
COLORADO
Smoky Hill River
Salina
Abilene
TOPEKA
Overland Park
Arkansas River
Garden City
Dodge City
Kansas "cowtowns" of the 1860-1870s were filled with longhorn cattle and wild cowboys.
Wichita
Verdigris River
Neosho River
Cimarron River
Liberal
OKLAHOMA

More tornadoes occur in Kansas than in any other state.

State insect: Honeybee

Thousands of longhorn cattle were driven from Texas to Kansas railroad stations.

State bird: Meadowlarks hide their nests in prairie grasses where millions of buffalo once roamed.

State flower: Sunflower

Kansas
Sunflower State

34th state • Statehood: January 29, 1861 • Population: 2,688,418 • Area: 82,282 square miles

Nutritious bluegrass near Lexington makes it the "Thoroughbred Capital of the World."

State bird: Kentucky cardinal

State tree: Tulip-poplar

In 1938, Bill Monroe and the Blue Grass Boys gave America a unique gift: bluegrass music.

Since 1875 the Kentucky Derby, a world-famous horse race, has been held each May at Churchill Downs.

Ft. Knox guards more gold than any other place in the world. No visitors!

OHIO
Covington
Ohio River
INDIANA
• Louisville
Salt River
▲ Fort Knox
★ FRANKFORT
• Lexington
• Owensboro
Rough River
▲ Birthplace of Abraham Lincoln (1809-1865), president of the Union during the Civil War.
Green River
▲ Mammoth Cave
Kentucky River
BIG Sandy River Tug Fork
WEST VIRGINIA
• Ashland
ILLINOIS
Lake Barkley
Birthplace of Jefferson Davis (1808-1889), president of the Confederacy during the Civil War.
Cumberland River
Appalachian Mountains
Black Mountain 4,145 ft.
MISSOURI
Mississippi River
Paducah
Kentucky Lake
Lake Cumberland
VIRGINIA
▲ Cumberland Gap
TENNESSEE

The Mammoth Cave system has 340 miles of underground passages. Over 200 animal species are found there.

Endangered species: Kentucky cave shrimp

swim in deep pools of the Mammoth Caves. Their small population is threatened by polluted groundwater.

Kentucky
Bluegrass State

State flower: Goldenrod graces the entire state with a golden glow.

Daniel Boone (1734-1820) led the first white settlers through the dangerous Cumberland Gap into Kentucky in 1775.

15th state • Statehood: June 1, 1792 • Population: 4,041,769 • Area: 40,411 square miles

State flower: Magnolia blossom

Endangered species: Louisiana black bear

State tree: Bald cypress

It hides in the dense underbrush of hardwood forests.

Spanish moss hangs from cypress and oak trees in bayous. Bayous are slow-moving streams in or out of swamps, lakes, or the ocean.

Mardi Gras is a holiday celebrated with parades, parties, feasts, and costume balls. Everyone wears a mask.

Birthplace of jazz and Louis "Satchmo" Armstrong (1900?-1971), world renowned for his trumpet sounds.

State insect: Honeybee

Louisiana crayfish are used in famous Cajun and Creole recipes.

Thousands of egrets, herons, and other birds flock to Avery Island and the swampy woods for safety.

The world's largest indoor arena, the Louisiana Superdome in New Orleans, has 95,427 seats.

State bird: Brown pelican. "A wonderful bird is the pelican! His bill will hold more than his belican!"—Dixon L. Merritt

Louisiana
Pelican state

ARKANSAS

Shreveport

Monroe

Driskill Mt. 535 ft.

Red River

Ouachita River

Mississippi River

TEXAS

Alexandria

MISSISSIPPI

Sabine River

Calcasieu River

Bayou Nezpique

Bayou Boeuf

Bayou Teche

Atchafalaya River

Pearl River

Lake Pontchartrain

BATON ROUGE

New Orleans

Bayou Lafourche

Lafayette

Lake Charles

Grand Lake

Avery Island

Calcasieu Lake

Sabine Lake

White Lake

Gulf of Mexico

State insect: Honeybee

Maine has over 2,500 lakes and 5,000 rivers or streams.

State animal: The moose symbolizes Maine's wildlife areas.

CANADA

St. John River

Allagash River

Aroostook River

CANADA

CANADA

Mt. Katahdin 5,268 ft.

Moosehead Lake

Endangered species: Furbish lousewort is found in the St. John River valley.

Maine's Atlantic coast is rocky and jagged.

Samantha Smith
Maine, USA

Yuri Andropov
Russia

In 1983, Samantha Smith (1972-1985), a schoolgirl from Augusta, wrote to the Soviet premier about her fear of war with his country. She was invited to visit Russia and became a symbol of what one person can do for world peace.

White Mountains

Piscataquis River

Grand Lake

Penobscot River

Machias River

Bangor

West Quoddy Head is the most easterly point of land in the U.S.A.

NEW HAMPSHIRE

Androscoggin River

Kennebec River

★ AUGUSTA

Lakes and coastline are ideal for sailing.

Sebago Lake

Portland

Atlantic Ocean

Kennebunkport

Portland Head Light, one of Maine's 62 lighthouses

Millions of pounds of tasty Maine lobsters are sold annually around the world.

State tree: White pine

State flower: White pine cone and tassel

State bird: Chickadee

Maine
Pine Tree State

23rd state • Statehood: March 15, 1820 • Population: 1,274,923 • Area: 35,387 square miles

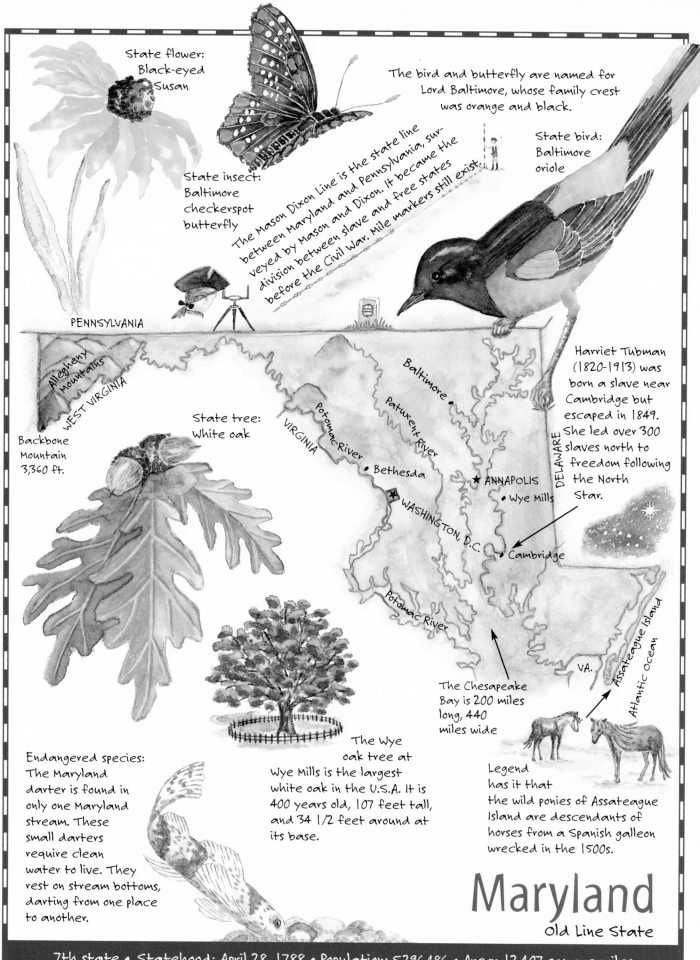

State flower: Black-eyed Susan

State insect: Baltimore checkerspot butterfly

The bird and butterfly are named for Lord Baltimore, whose family crest was orange and black.

State bird: Baltimore oriole

The Mason Dixon Line is the state line between Maryland and Pennsylvania, surveyed by Mason and Dixon. It became the division between slave and free states before the Civil War. Mile markers still exist.

PENNSYLVANIA

Allegheny Mountains

WEST VIRGINIA

Backbone Mountain 3,360 ft.

State tree: White oak

VIRGINIA

Potomac River

Baltimore •

Patuxent River

• Bethesda

★ ANNAPOLIS

WASHINGTON, D.C. ★

DELAWARE

• Wye Mills

• Cambridge

Harriet Tubman (1820-1913) was born a slave near Cambridge but escaped in 1849. She led over 300 slaves north to freedom following the North Star.

Potomac River

The Chesapeake Bay is 200 miles long, 440 miles wide

VA.

Assateague Island

Atlantic Ocean

The Wye oak tree at Wye Mills is the largest white oak in the U.S.A. It is 400 years old, 107 feet tall, and 34 1/2 feet around at its base.

Endangered species: The Maryland darter is found in only one Maryland stream. These small darters require clean water to live. They rest on stream bottoms, darting from one place to another.

Legend has it that the wild ponies of Assateague Island are descendants of horses from a Spanish galleon wrecked in the 1500s.

Maryland
Old Line State

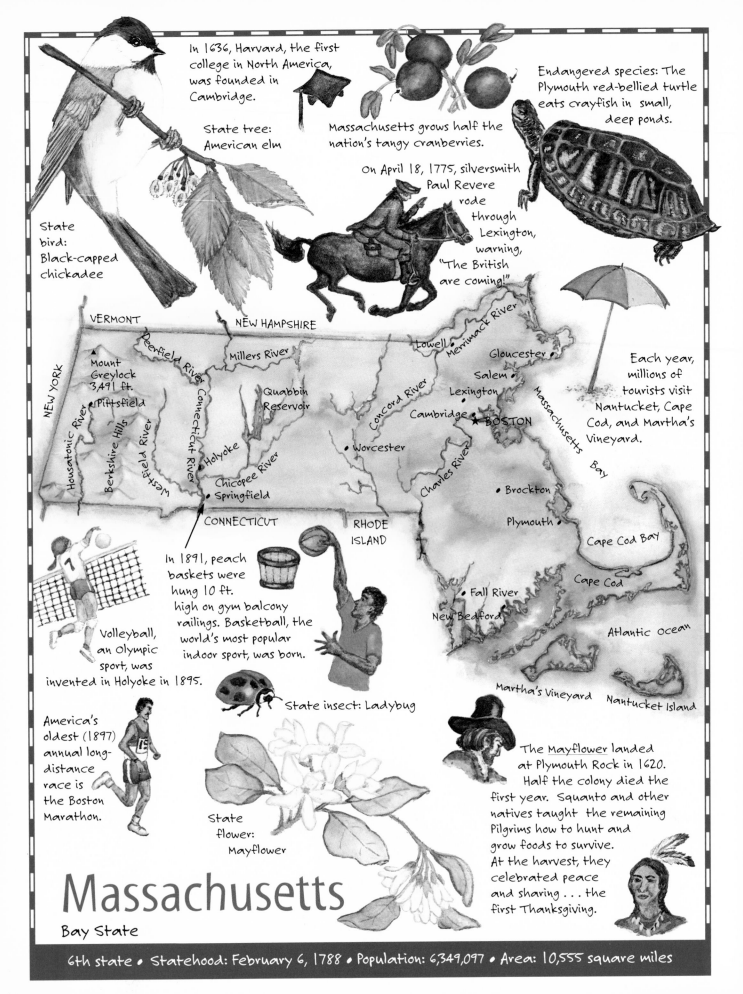

State bird: Black-capped chickadee

In 1636, Harvard, the first college in North America, was founded in Cambridge.

State tree: American elm

Massachusetts grows half the nation's tangy cranberries.

On April 18, 1775, silversmith Paul Revere rode through Lexington, warning, "The British are coming!"

Endangered species: The Plymouth red-bellied turtle eats crayfish in small, deep ponds.

Each year, millions of tourists visit Nantucket, Cape Cod, and Martha's Vineyard.

VERMONT
NEW HAMPSHIRE
NEW YORK
Mount Greylock 3,491 ft.
Deerfield River
Millers River
Pittsfield
Housatonic River
Berkshire Hills
Westfield River
Connecticut River
Quabbin Reservoir
Holyoke
Chicopee River
Springfield
CONNECTICUT
Lowell
Merrimack River
Gloucester
Salem
Lexington
Concord River
Cambridge
★ BOSTON
Worcester
Charles River
RHODE ISLAND
Massachusetts Bay
Brockton
Plymouth
Cape Cod Bay
Cape Cod
Fall River
New Bedford
Atlantic Ocean
Martha's Vineyard
Nantucket Island

Volleyball, an Olympic sport, was invented in Holyoke in 1895.

In 1891, peach baskets were hung 10 ft. high on gym balcony railings. Basketball, the world's most popular indoor sport, was born.

State insect: Ladybug

America's oldest (1897) annual long-distance race is the Boston Marathon.

State flower: Mayflower

The Mayflower landed at Plymouth Rock in 1620. Half the colony died the first year. Squanto and other natives taught the remaining Pilgrims how to hunt and grow foods to survive. At the harvest, they celebrated peace and sharing . . . the first Thanksgiving.

Massachusetts
Bay State

6th state • Statehood: February 6, 1788 • Population: 6,349,097 • Area: 10,555 square miles

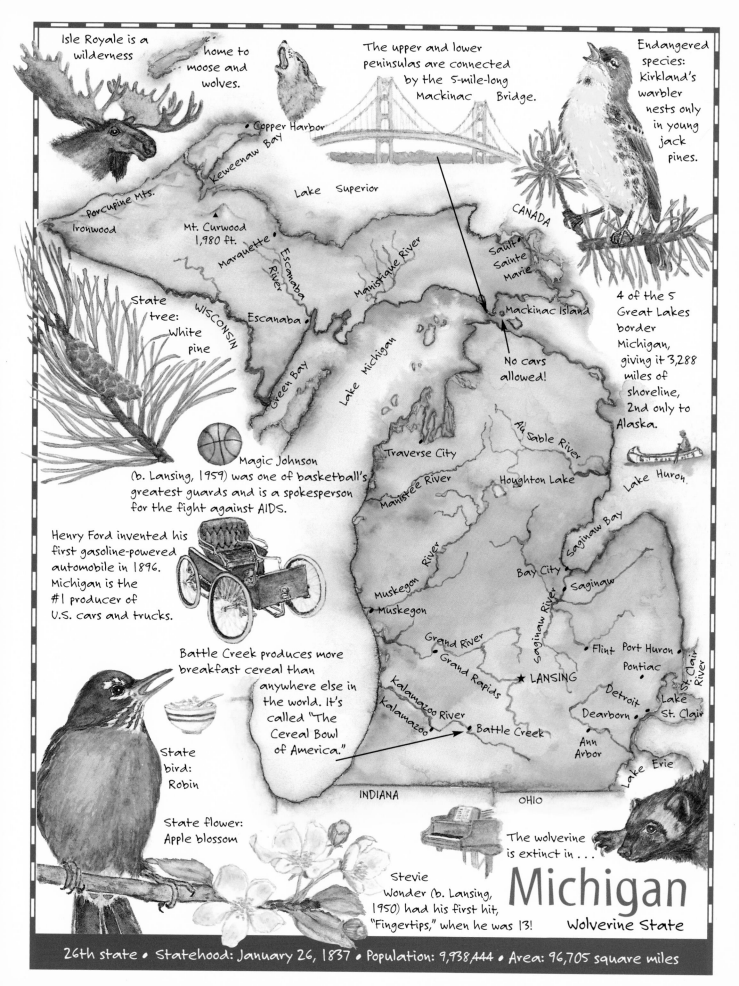

Isle Royale is a wilderness home to moose and wolves.

The upper and lower peninsulas are connected by the 5-mile-long Mackinac Bridge.

Endangered species: Kirkland's warbler nests only in young jack pines.

Copper Harbor

Keweenaw Bay

Lake Superior

CANADA

Porcupine Mts.

Ironwood

Mt. Curwood 1,980 ft.

Marquette

Escanaba River

Sault Sainte Marie

Mackinac Island

No cars allowed!

4 of the 5 Great Lakes border Michigan, giving it 3,288 miles of shoreline, 2nd only to Alaska.

State tree: White pine

WISCONSIN

Escanaba

Manistique River

Lake Michigan

Green Bay

Magic Johnson (b. Lansing, 1959) was one of basketball's greatest guards and is a spokesperson for the fight against AIDS.

Traverse City

Au Sable River

Houghton Lake

Lake Huron

Manistee River

River

Saginaw Bay

Henry Ford invented his first gasoline-powered automobile in 1896. Michigan is the #1 producer of U.S. cars and trucks.

Muskegon River

Muskegon

Bay City

Saginaw

Saginaw River

Battle Creek produces more breakfast cereal than anywhere else in the world. It's called "The Cereal Bowl of America."

Grand River

Grand Rapids

LANSING

Flint

Port Huron

Pontiac

St. Clair River

Kalamazoo River

Kalamazoo

Battle Creek

Detroit

Lake St. Clair

Dearborn

State bird: Robin

Ann Arbor

State flower: Apple blossom

INDIANA

OHIO

Lake Erie

The wolverine is extinct in . . .

Stevie Wonder (b. Lansing, 1950) had his first hit, "Fingertips," when he was 13!

Michigan
Wolverine State

26th state • Statehood: January 26, 1837 • Population: 9,938,444 • Area: 96,705 square miles

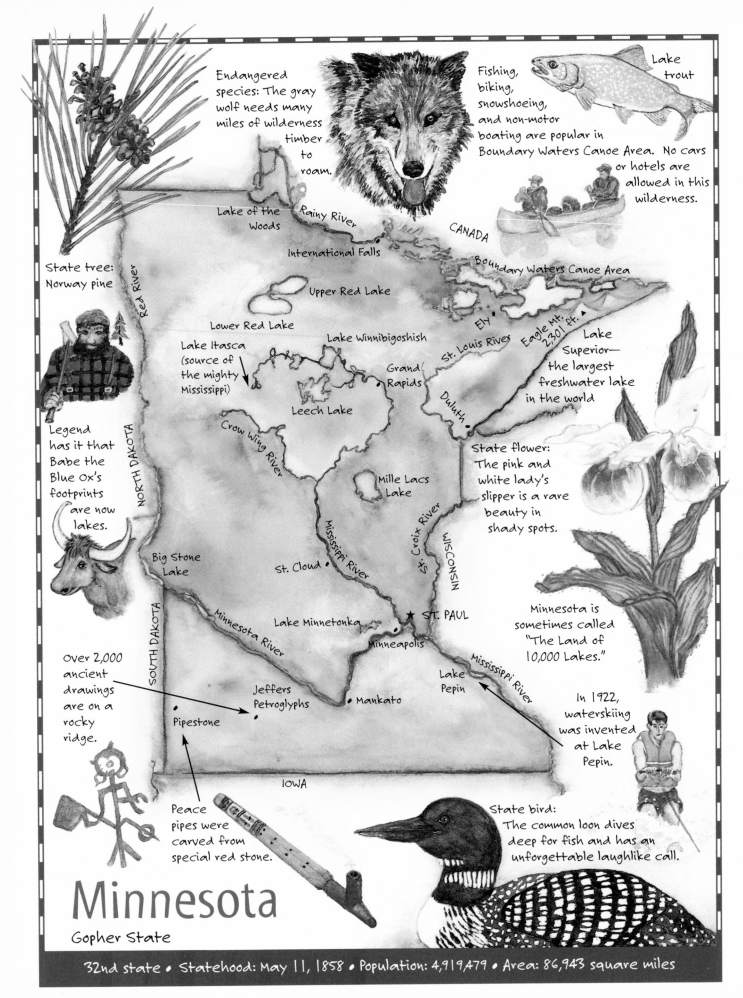

Endangered species: The gray wolf needs many miles of wilderness timber to roam.

Lake trout

Fishing, biking, snowshoeing, and non-motor boating are popular in Boundary Waters Canoe Area. No cars or hotels are allowed in this wilderness.

CANADA

Lake of the Woods

Rainy River

International Falls

Boundary Waters Canoe Area

State tree: Norway pine

Red River

Upper Red Lake

Lower Red Lake

Lake Winnibigoshish

Ely

St. Louis River

Eagle Mt. 2,301 ft.

Lake Superior— the largest freshwater lake in the world

Lake Itasca (source of the mighty Mississippi)

Grand Rapids

Duluth

Leech Lake

Crow Wing River

Legend has it that Babe the Blue Ox's footprints are now lakes.

NORTH DAKOTA

Mille Lacs Lake

State flower: The pink and white lady's slipper is a rare beauty in shady spots.

Mississippi River

St. Croix River

WISCONSIN

Big Stone Lake

St. Cloud

Minnesota is sometimes called "The Land of 10,000 Lakes."

SOUTH DAKOTA

Minnesota River

Lake Minnetonka

★ ST. PAUL

Minneapolis

Lake Pepin

Mississippi River

In 1922, waterskiing was invented at Lake Pepin.

Over 2,000 ancient drawings are on a rocky ridge.

Jeffers Petroglyphs

Mankato

Pipestone

IOWA

Peace pipes were carved from special red stone.

State bird: The common loon dives deep for fish and has an unforgettable laughlike call.

Minnesota

Gopher State

32nd state • Statehood: May 11, 1858 • Population: 4,919,479 • Area: 86,943 square miles

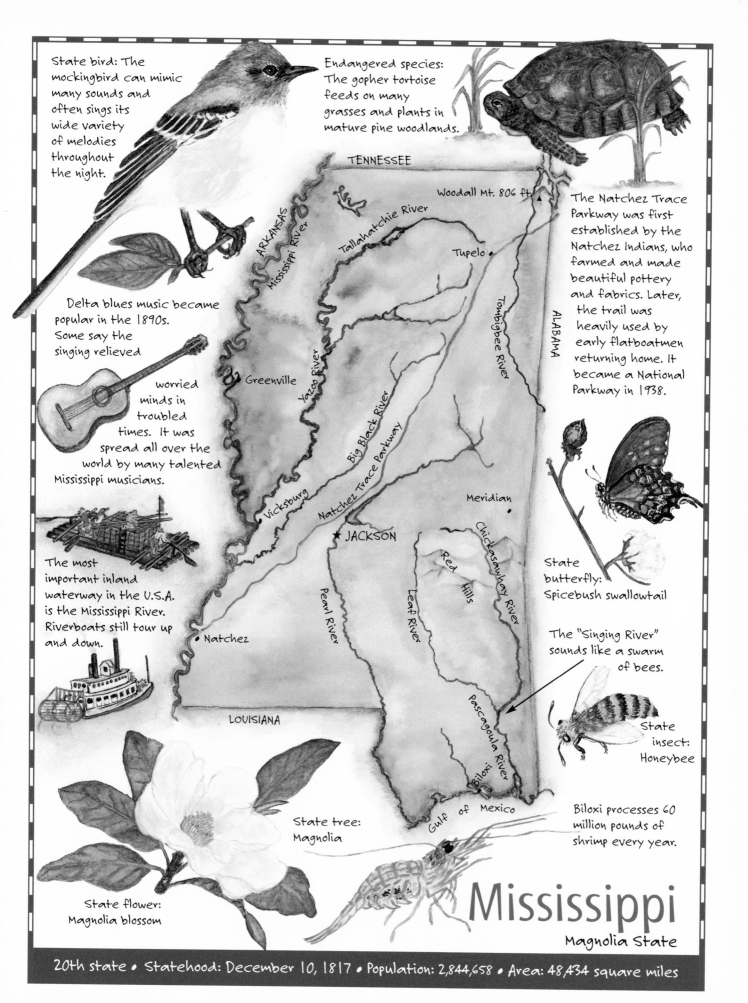

State bird: The mockingbird can mimic many sounds and often sings its wide variety of melodies throughout the night.

Endangered species: The gopher tortoise feeds on many grasses and plants in mature pine woodlands.

TENNESSEE

Woodall Mt. 806 ft.

ARKANSAS

Mississippi River

Tallahatchie River

Tupelo

ALABAMA

Tombigbee River

The Natchez Trace Parkway was first established by the Natchez Indians, who farmed and made beautiful pottery and fabrics. Later, the trail was heavily used by early flatboatmen returning home. It became a National Parkway in 1938.

Delta blues music became popular in the 1890s. Some say the singing relieved worried minds in troubled times. It was spread all over the world by many talented Mississippi musicians.

Greenville

Yazoo River

Big Black River

Natchez Trace Parkway

Vicksburg

The most important inland waterway in the U.S.A. is the Mississippi River. Riverboats still tour up and down.

★ JACKSON

Meridian

Chickasawhay River

Red Hills

Natchez

Pearl River

Leaf River

State butterfly: Spicebush swallowtail

The "Singing River" sounds like a swarm of bees.

LOUISIANA

Pascagoula River

State insect: Honeybee

Biloxi

Gulf of Mexico

Biloxi processes 60 million pounds of shrimp every year.

State tree: Magnolia

State flower: Magnolia blossom

Mississippi
Magnolia State

20th state • Statehood: December 10, 1817 • Population: 2,844,658 • Area: 48,434 square miles

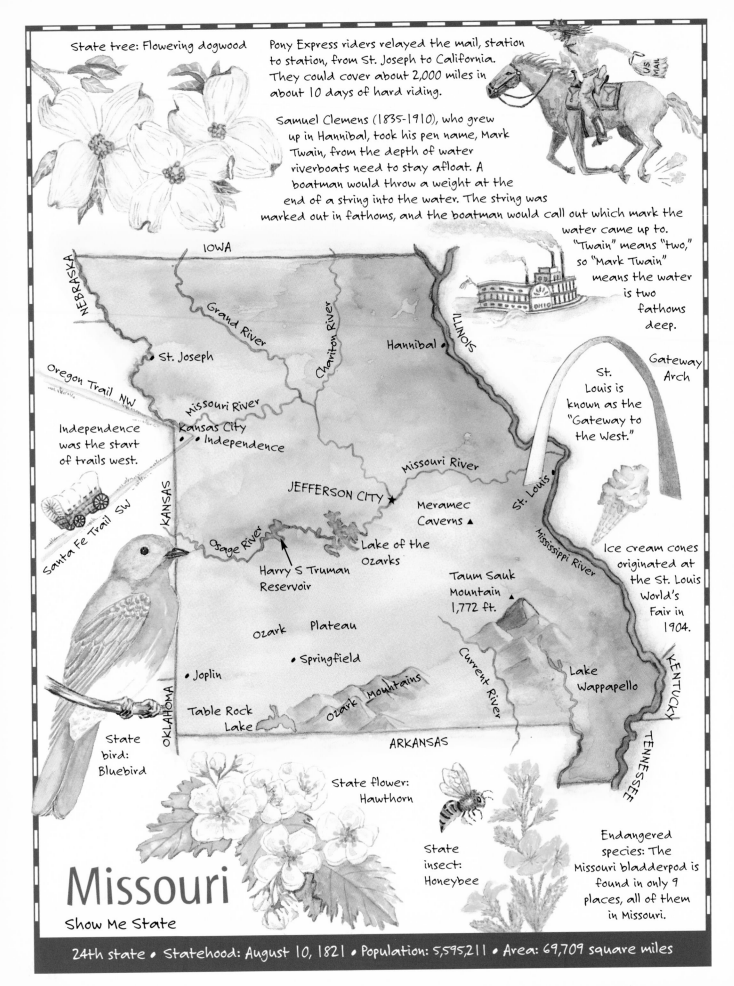

State tree: Flowering dogwood

Pony Express riders relayed the mail, station to station, from St. Joseph to California. They could cover about 2,000 miles in about 10 days of hard riding.

Samuel Clemens (1835-1910), who grew up in Hannibal, took his pen name, Mark Twain, from the depth of water riverboats need to stay afloat. A boatman would throw a weight at the end of a string into the water. The string was marked out in fathoms, and the boatman would call out which mark the water came up to. "Twain" means "two," so "Mark Twain" means the water is two fathoms deep.

IOWA

NEBRASKA

Grand River

Chariton River

ILLINOIS

Hannibal

St. Joseph

Oregon Trail NW

Missouri River

Gateway Arch

St. Louis is known as the "Gateway to the West."

Independence was the start of trails west.

Kansas City
• Independence

KANSAS

Santa Fe Trail SW

Missouri River

JEFFERSON CITY ★

Meramec Caverns ▲

St. Louis •

Mississippi River

Ice cream cones originated at the St. Louis World's Fair in 1904.

Osage River

Harry S Truman Reservoir

Lake of the Ozarks

Taum Sauk Mountain 1,772 ft. ▲

Ozark Plateau

• Springfield

Current River

Lake Wappapello

KENTUCKY

State bird: Bluebird

OKLAHOMA

• Joplin

Table Rock Lake

Ozark Mountains

ARKANSAS

TENNESSEE

State flower: Hawthorn

State insect: Honeybee

Endangered species: The Missouri bladderpod is found in only 9 places, all of them in Missouri.

Missouri

Show Me State

State bird: Meadowlark

State tree: Ponderosa pine

Chief Joseph led his Nez Percé tribe over 1,600 miles on an epic retreat from U.S. troops. In October 1877, he surrendered at Bear Paw, saying, "I will fight no more . . . forever."

A Native American sign for "peace"

Endangered species: The grizzly bear is also the state animal.

Home to grizzly bears and over 50 glaciers.

Glacier National Park

CANADA

Flathead Lake

Continental Divide

Rocky Mountains

Milk River

Bear Paw Battlefield

Missouri River

IDAHO

Missoula

Great Falls

Missouri River

Fort Peck Lake

HELENA ★

NORTH DAKOTA

Musselshell River

The Lewis and Clark Expedition traveled the great Montana rivers. York, Clark's servant, was the first black man many Native Americans had ever seen.

Butte

Yellowstone River

Bozeman

Billings

Pompey's Pillar

Custer's Battlefield

Madison River

Granite Peak 12,799 ft.

Yellowstone Park

WYOMING

This rock formation was named for Sacajawea's son "Pomp." William Clark carved "Wᴹ Clark July 25, 1806" in the rock. It's still there.

Site of "Custer's Last Stand" where Sioux and Cheyenne killed all 210 of Custer's troops, June 25, 1876. Only one wounded horse survived.

Big Sky Country

Almost every Montana town still has an "Old West" rodeo.

State flower: Bitterroot

Montana
Treasure State

41st state • Statehood: November 8, 1889 • Population: 902,195 • Area: 147,046 square miles

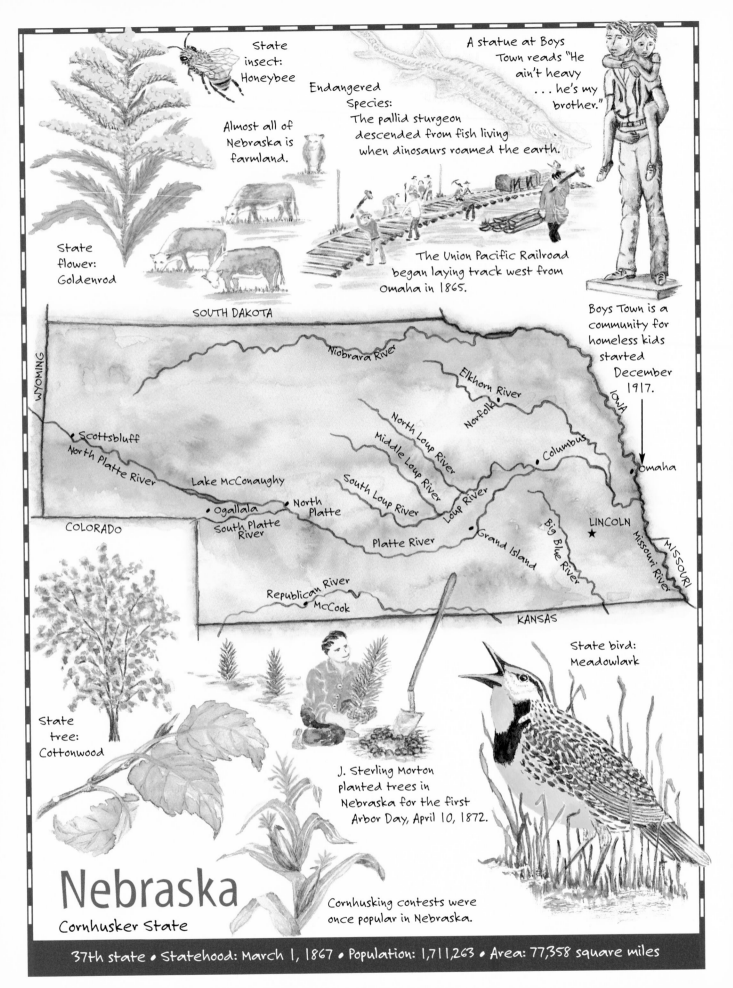

State insect: Honeybee

Endangered Species:
The pallid sturgeon descended from fish living when dinosaurs roamed the earth.

A statue at Boys Town reads "He ain't heavy . . . he's my brother."

Almost all of Nebraska is farmland.

State flower: Goldenrod

The Union Pacific Railroad began laying track west from Omaha in 1865.

Boys Town is a community for homeless kids started December 1917.

SOUTH DAKOTA

WYOMING

Niobrara River

Elkhorn River

Norfolk

North Loup River

Middle Loup River

Scottsbluff

North Platte River

Columbus

IOWA

Lake McConaughy

South Loup River

Loup River

Omaha

Ogallala

North Platte

South Platte River

LINCOLN

Big Blue River

Missouri River

MISSOURI

COLORADO

Platte River

Grand Island

Republican River

McCook

KANSAS

State tree: Cottonwood

J. Sterling Morton planted trees in Nebraska for the first Arbor Day, April 10, 1872.

State bird: Meadowlark

Nebraska
Cornhusker State

Cornhusking contests were once popular in Nebraska.

37th state • Statehood: March 1, 1867 • Population: 1,711,263 • Area: 77,358 square miles

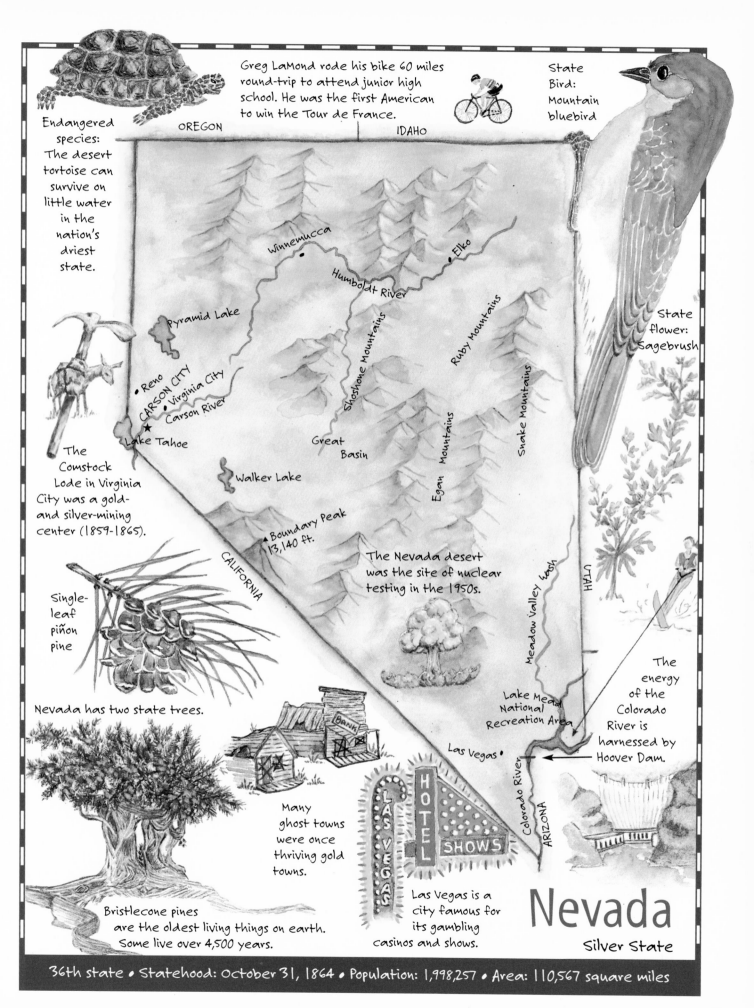

Endangered species: The desert tortoise can survive on little water in the nation's driest state.

Greg LaMond rode his bike 60 miles round-trip to attend junior high school. He was the first American to win the Tour de France.

State Bird: Mountain bluebird

OREGON

IDAHO

State flower: Sagebrush

Winnemucca

Elko

Humboldt River

Pyramid Lake

Shoshone Mountains

Ruby Mountains

Snake Mountains

Reno
CARSON CITY
Virginia City
Carson River

Lake Tahoe

Egan Mountains

Great Basin

The Comstock Lode in Virginia City was a gold- and silver-mining center (1859-1865).

Walker Lake

Boundary Peak 13,140 ft.

CALIFORNIA

The Nevada desert was the site of nuclear testing in the 1950s.

Single-leaf piñon pine

Nevada has two state trees.

Meadow Valley Wash

UTAH

The energy of the Colorado River is harnessed by Hoover Dam.

Lake Mead National Recreation Area

Las Vegas

Many ghost towns were once thriving gold towns.

Colorado River

ARIZONA

LAS VEGAS
HOTEL
SHOWS

Las Vegas is a city famous for its gambling casinos and shows.

Bristlecone pines are the oldest living things on earth. Some live over 4,500 years.

Nevada
Silver State

36th state • Statehood: October 31, 1864 • Population: 1,998,257 • Area: 110,567 square miles

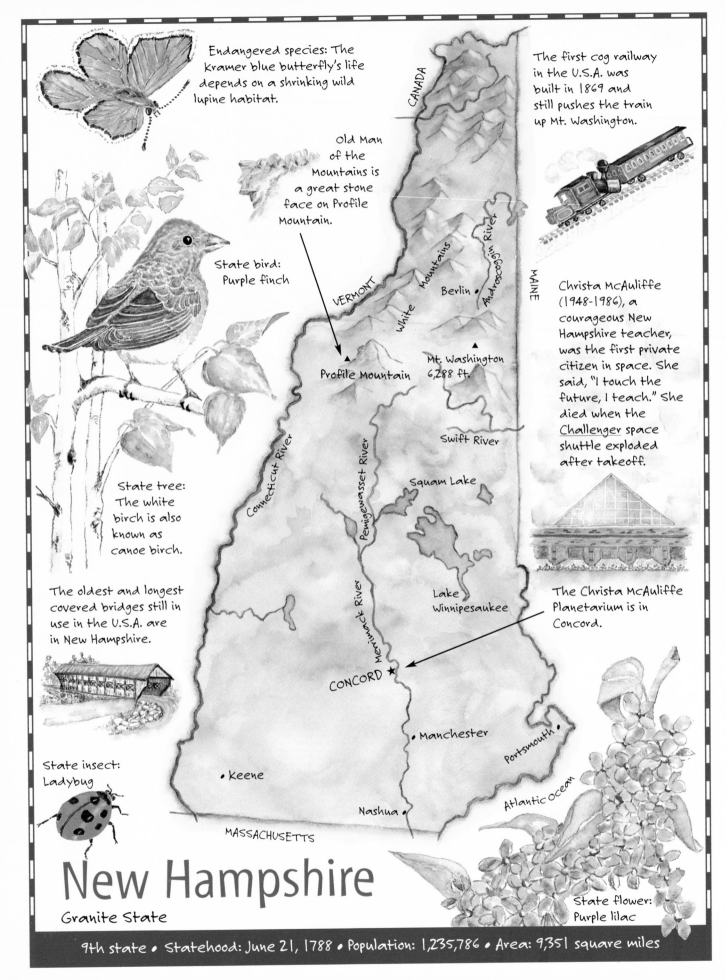

Endangered species: The Kramer blue butterfly's life depends on a shrinking wild lupine habitat.

The first cog railway in the U.S.A. was built in 1869 and still pushes the train up Mt. Washington.

Old Man of the Mountains is a great stone face on Profile Mountain.

State bird: Purple finch

CANADA

VERMONT

White Mountains

Androscoggin River

Berlin

MAINE

Mt. Washington 6,288 ft.

Profile Mountain

Swift River

Christa McAuliffe (1948-1986), a courageous New Hampshire teacher, was the first private citizen in space. She said, "I touch the future, I teach." She died when the <u>Challenger</u> space shuttle exploded after takeoff.

State tree: The white birch is also known as canoe birch.

Connecticut River

Pemigewasset River

Squam Lake

Lake Winnipesaukee

The oldest and longest covered bridges still in use in the U.S.A. are in New Hampshire.

The Christa McAuliffe Planetarium is in Concord.

Merrimack River

CONCORD ★

State insect: Ladybug

• Manchester

Portsmouth

• Keene

Atlantic Ocean

Nashua •

MASSACHUSETTS

New Hampshire

Granite State

State flower: Purple lilac

9th state • Statehood: June 21, 1788 • Population: 1,235,786 • Area: 9,351 square miles

State bird:
Goldfinch

State tree:
Red oak bark is rich
in tannin, used for
tanning leather.

The Garden State is famous for
its Jersey tomatoes.

New Jersey is a leader in producing chemicals.

State dinosaur:
Hadrosaurus, the
first dinosaur
skeleton
discovered in North
America, was found
near Haddonfield
in 1858.

The Sandy Hook
Lighthouse has
been guiding ships
into port since
1763.

Many people
vacation on the
white sandy
beaches of the
Jersey shore.

Endangered species:
Roseate tern

It needs
isolated
beaches for
concealed
nests.

State insect:
Honeybees are
vital for
pollinating
gardens.

The Pine Barrens
is a wilderness of
bogs, salt marshes,
and swamps.

Atlantic City is
famous for its wooden
boardwalk and
saltwater taffy.

State flower:
Violet

PENNSYLVANIA

NEW YORK

Appalachian Mountains

Musconetcong River

Lake Hopatcong

Passaic River

Hackensack River

Hudson River

Newark

Hoboken
Jersey City

Piedmont Plateau

Princeton

★ TRENTON

Delaware River

Camden

Haddonfield

Tom's River

Mullica River

Great Egg Harbor River

DELAWARE

Delaware Bay

Cape May

Jersey Shore Resorts

Atlantic Ocean

New Jersey
Garden State

State tree: Piñon pine

Gallup hosts the Intertribal Indian Ceremonial every August.

Endangered species: New Mexican ridgenose rattlesnakes hide out in remote pine-oak woodlands.

Hot air balloons from all over the world come to Albuquerque in mid-October.

Shiprock, or Tsé Bit'a'i, is a rock formation sacred to the Navajo.

State insect: Tarantula hawk wasps lay eggs inside spiders.

New Mexico grows the most chilies in the U.S.A.

In 1950, a bear cub was rescued from a forest fire; he became Smoky the Bear.

Santa Fe was founded in 1610 and is the oldest state capital.

The sand dunes are so white they glisten like snow fields.

State flower: Yucca

At dusk, tens of thousands of bats emerge from limestone caverns in 24 miles of passages to feast on millions of bugs. There are many caves. The Big Room is the largest natural cave in the world.

State bird: The roadrunner prefers to run (15 m.p.h.) rather than fly.

UTAH
Four Corners
COLORADO
OKLAHOMA
Farmington
San Juan River
Wheeler Peak 13,161 ft.
Chaco Culture National Historic Park
Coyote
Taos
Canadian River
Los Alamos
★ SANTA FE
Gallup
Continental Divide
Albuquerque
Pecos River
Clovis
Mogollon
Rocky Mountains
Lincoln National Forest
Gila River
Rio Grande
Roswell
Silver City
White Sands National Monument
Carlsbad Caverns
Las Cruces
ARIZONA
Columbus
TEXAS
MEXICO

New Mexico
Land of Enchantment

47th state • Statehood: January 6, 1912 • Population: 1,819,046 • Area: 121,598 square miles

Lake Placid was the site of the 1932 and the 1980 Winter Olympics.

State Flower: Rose

Mary Jemison was a white child captured by a Seneca tribe in 1755. She refused later offers to return to a white settlement.

Endangered species: The American hart's-tongue fern grows in the cool, moist soil of limestone sinkholes.

State insect: Ladybug

The Statue of Liberty was a gift from France in 1884. It stands in New York Harbor.

Canada and the U.S.A. share the world's most famous waterfall.

CANADA

Lake Champlain

Lake Placid

Mt. Marcy 5,344 ft.

CANADA

Thousand Islands

Lake George

Adirondack Mountains

VERMONT

Lake Ontario

Niagara Falls

Syracuse

Oneida Lake

Mohawk River

Rochester

Utica

Buffalo
East Aurora

Genesee River

Cooperstown

Susquehanna River

ALBANY

MASSACHUSETTS

Lake Erie

Finger Lakes

Catskill Mountains

Hudson River

Poughkeepsie

CONNECTICUT

Elmira

Binghamton

PENNSYLVANIA

West Point

Cooperstown is home to the National Baseball Hall of Fame.

State bird: Bluebird

Coney Island is a beach resort known for its boardwalk and hot dogs.

NEW JERSEY

New York City

Long Island Sound

Long Island

RADIO CITY

Staten Island

Atlantic Ocean

Opened in 1932, in downtown New York City, this theater seats 5,883.

From 1892 to 1954, over 12 million immigrants passed through Ellis Island Center.

State tree: The sugar maple is the source of maple syrup and candy, as well as blazing autumn colors.

The United Nations headquarters are in New York City.

New York

Empire State

11th state • Statehood: July 26, 1788 • Population: 18,976,457 • Area: 54,471 square miles

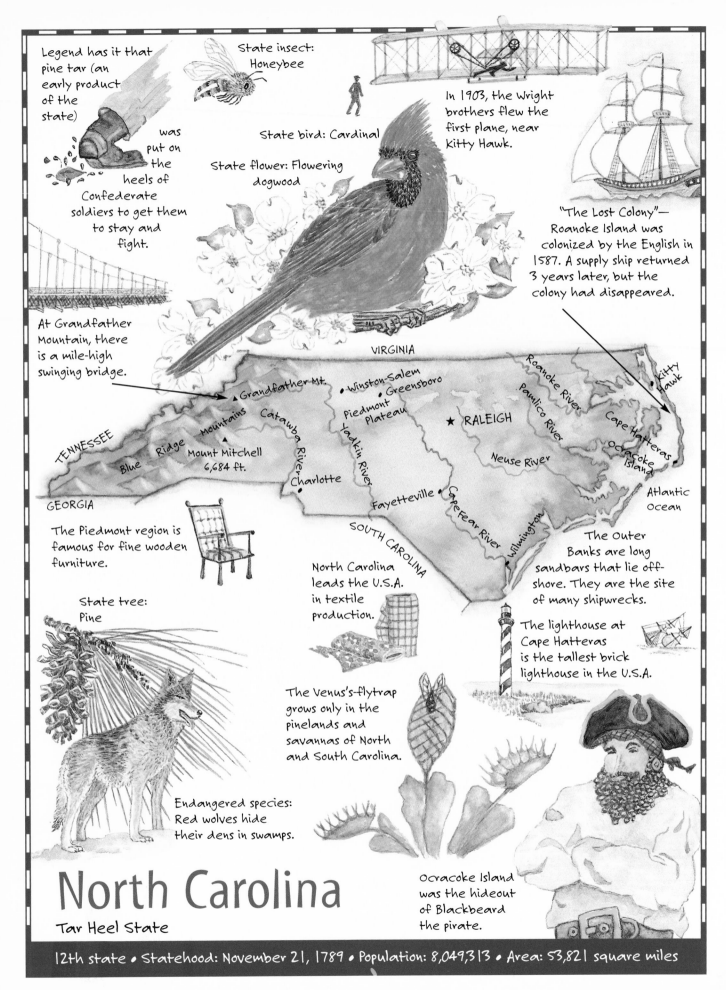

Legend has it that pine tar (an early product of the state) was put on the heels of Confederate soldiers to get them to stay and fight.

State insect: Honeybee

State bird: Cardinal

State flower: Flowering dogwood

In 1903, the Wright brothers flew the first plane, near Kitty Hawk.

"The Lost Colony"— Roanoke Island was colonized by the English in 1587. A supply ship returned 3 years later, but the colony had disappeared.

At Grandfather Mountain, there is a mile-high swinging bridge.

VIRGINIA

Grandfather Mt. • Winston-Salem • Greensboro
Piedmont Plateau
Roanoke River
Kitty Hawk
Pamlico River
Cape Hatteras
★ RALEIGH
Ocracoke Island
Blue Ridge Mountains Catawba River Yadkin River
Mount Mitchell 6,684 ft.
Neuse River
TENNESSEE
Charlotte
Fayetteville • Cape Fear River
Atlantic Ocean
GEORGIA
Wilmington
SOUTH CAROLINA

The Piedmont region is famous for fine wooden furniture.

North Carolina leads the U.S.A. in textile production.

The Outer Banks are long sandbars that lie off-shore. They are the site of many shipwrecks.

State tree: Pine

The lighthouse at Cape Hatteras is the tallest brick lighthouse in the U.S.A.

The Venus's-flytrap grows only in the pinelands and savannas of North and South Carolina.

Endangered species: Red wolves hide their dens in swamps.

North Carolina

Tar Heel State

Ocracoke Island was the hideout of Blackbeard the pirate.

12th state • Statehood: November 21, 1789 • Population: 8,049,313 • Area: 53,821 square miles

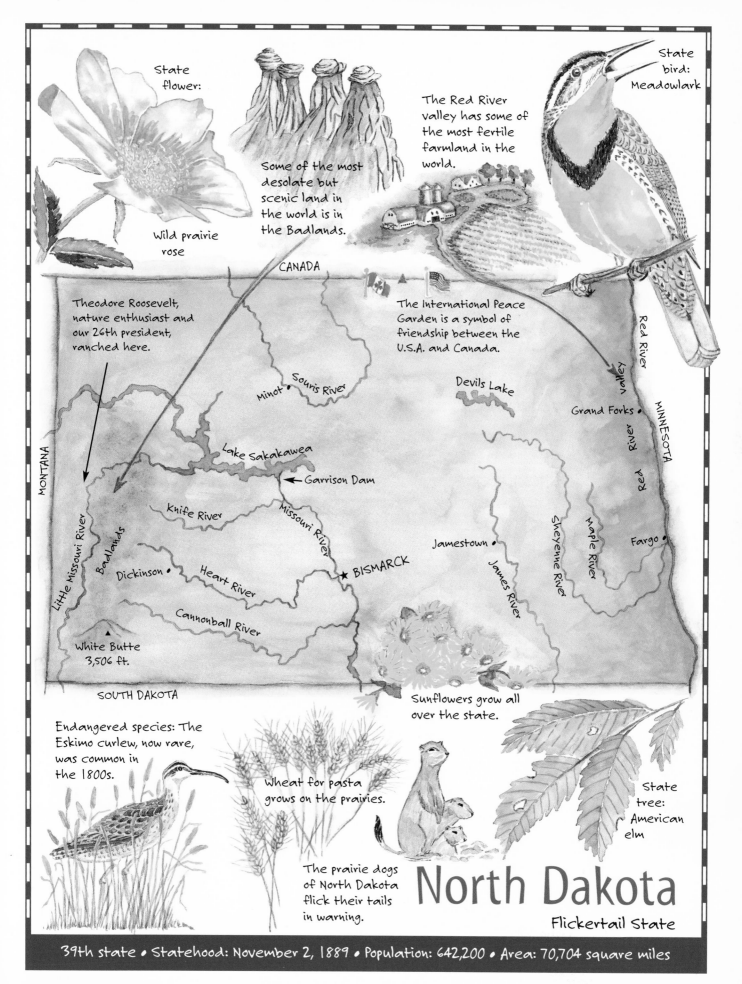

State flower:

Wild prairie rose

Some of the most desolate but scenic land in the world is in the Badlands.

The Red River valley has some of the most fertile farmland in the world.

State bird: Meadowlark

Theodore Roosevelt, nature enthusiast and our 26th president, ranched here.

The International Peace Garden is a symbol of friendship between the U.S.A. and Canada.

CANADA

Red River Valley

MINNESOTA

Minot • Souris River

Devils Lake

Grand Forks •

Red River

MONTANA

Lake Sakakawea

Garrison Dam

Knife River

Little Missouri River

Badlands

Dickinson •

Heart River

Missouri River

BISMARCK ★

Jamestown •

Sheyenne River

Maple River

Fargo •

James River

Cannonball River

White Butte 3,506 ft.

SOUTH DAKOTA

Sunflowers grow all over the state.

Endangered species: The Eskimo curlew, now rare, was common in the 1800s.

Wheat for pasta grows on the prairies.

State tree: American elm

The prairie dogs of North Dakota flick their tails in warning.

North Dakota

Flickertail State

39th state • Statehood: November 2, 1889 • Population: 642,200 • Area: 70,704 square miles

Endangered species: The lakeside daisy grows in limestone quarries.

John Chapman (Johnny Appleseed) planted hundreds of acres of apple orchards in Ohio.

Raw materials imported on Ohio's rail, water, and truck routes are manufactured into products and exported on the same routes.

The Pro Football Hall of Fame is in Canton.

MICHIGAN

Toledo

Lake Erie
Cleveland

Maumee River

Sandusky River

Sandusky

Akron

Cuyahoga River

Youngstown

PENNSYLVANIA

Seven U.S. presidents were born in Ohio: Grant Hayes Garfield Harrison McKinley Taft Harding

About 2,000 years ago, Indian Mound Builders came to the Ohio Valley and shaped over 10,000 burial mounds. The Serpentine Mound near Hillsboro is more than 1/4 mile long.

INDIANA

Campbell Hill 1,550 ft.

Canton

SEAL OF THE PRESIDENT OF THE UNITED STATES

COLUMBUS

Great Miami River

Dayton

Little Miami River

Scioto River

Muskingum River

Ohio River

The Ohio River is navigable all year long.

Marietta

It empties into the Mississippi.

Cincinnati

Hillsboro

WEST VIRGINIA

KENTUCKY

Ohio River

State bird: Cardinal

State flower: Scarlet carnation

An Ohio architect, Maya Ying Lin, designed the Vietnam Memorial in Washington, D.C.

State tree: Buckeye

Ohio
Buckeye State

State insect: Ladybug

17th state • Statehood: March 1, 1803 • Population: 11,353,140 • Area: 44,828 square miles

Oil is found in every Oklahoma county. There is even an oil pump on the front lawn of the state capitol.

Endangered species: Piping plovers nest on sandy river beaches.

The National Cowboy Hall of Fame is in Oklahoma City.

"The Trail of Tears"— Between 1830 and 1842, Native Americans were made to travel over 1,000 miles from the southeast to resettle in Oklahoma.

Will Rogers (1879-1935) entertained with rope tricks and witty remarks. He said, "I never met a man I didn't like."

COLORADO
KANSAS
NEW MEXICO
Black Mesa 4,973 ft.
North Canadian River
TEXAS
MISSOURI

State bird: Scissor-tailed flycatcher

The Red River's color comes from the clay and minerals in the water.

Cimarron River
Chisholm Trail
Enid
Arkansas River
Oolagah Lake
Tulsa
Guthrie
Muskogee
Washita River
OKLAHOMA CITY
Canadian River
ARKANSAS
Wichita Mountains
Ouachita Mountains
Red River
Lake Texoma
TEXAS

State tree: Redbud

In the 1870s, the Chisholm Trail was a major route to drive cattle north to the Kansas railroads.

State flower: Mistletoe (a tree parasite)

At noon on April 22, a pistol shot started the 1889 land run. 50,000 settlers moved into Oklahoma overnight. Some folks snuck in "sooner," before the land was opened.

State wildflower: Blanketflower

Oklahoma
Sooner State

46th state • Statehood: November 16, 1907 • Population: 3,450,654 • Area: 69,903 square miles

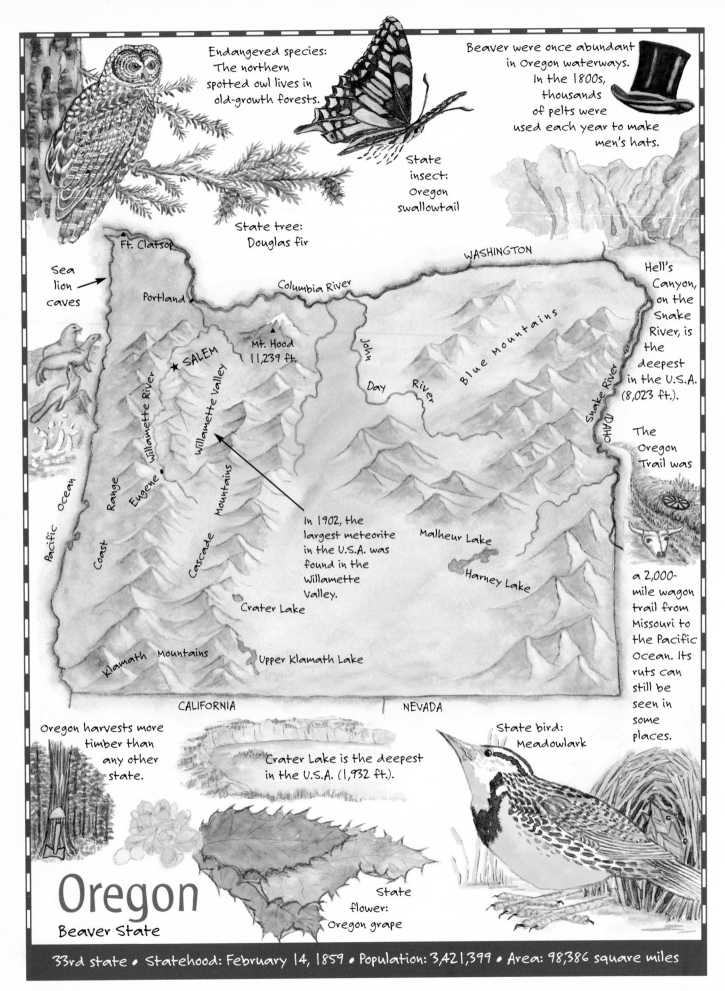

Endangered species: The northern spotted owl lives in old-growth forests.

State insect: Oregon swallowtail

Beaver were once abundant in Oregon waterways. In the 1800s, thousands of pelts were used each year to make men's hats.

State tree: Douglas fir

Ft. Clatsop

Sea lion caves

WASHINGTON

Portland

Columbia River

Hell's Canyon, on the Snake River, is the deepest in the U.S.A. (8,023 ft.).

Mt. Hood 11,239 ft.

★ SALEM

Willamette River

Willamette Valley

John

Day

River

Blue Mountains

Snake River

IDAHO

Pacific Ocean

Coast Range

Eugene

Cascade Mountains

The Oregon Trail was

In 1902, the largest meteorite in the U.S.A. was found in the Willamette Valley.

Malheur Lake

Harney Lake

a 2,000-mile wagon trail from Missouri to the Pacific Ocean. Its ruts can still be seen in some places.

Crater Lake

Klamath Mountains

Upper Klamath Lake

CALIFORNIA

NEVADA

State bird: Meadowlark

Oregon harvests more timber than any other state.

Crater Lake is the deepest in the U.S.A. (1,932 ft.).

Oregon
Beaver State

State flower: Oregon grape

33rd state • Statehood: February 14, 1859 • Population: 3,421,399 • Area: 98,386 square miles

State flower: Mountain laurel

State insect: Firefly

Endangered species: Northern riffle shell mussels like streams with firm packed sand.

German settlers, called Pennsylvania Dutch, are still known for their simple ways, folk art, and farming.

Benjamin Franklin, author, inventor, scientist, and statesman, lived in Pennsylvania.

Lake Erie
Erie

NEW YORK

OHIO

Steel is an important industry.

Allegheny River

Allegheny Mountains

West Susquehanna River

Scranton

Appalachian Mountains

World's largest chocolate factory

Bethlehem

Susquehanna River

Delaware Water Gap

NEW JERSEY

Delaware River

Ohio River

Pittsburgh

Altoona

Johnstown

Monongahela River

Juniata River

Hershey

HARRISBURG

Reading

Valley Forge ▲

Philadelphia

Mt. Davis ▲ 3,213 ft.

Gettysburg

DELAWARE

WEST VIRGINIA

MARYLAND

State tree: Hemlock

The Declaration of Independence and the U.S. Constitution were written in Philadelphia. It's also the home of the Liberty Bell.

We the People Article I

The Battle of Gettysburg was the turning point of the Civil War.

JULY 4, 1776

Center or keystone of the original 13 colonies.

State bird: Ruffed grouse

Pennsylvania
Keystone State

2nd state • Statehood: December 12, 1787 • Population: 12,281,054 • Area: 46,058 square miles

MASSACHUSETTS

Woonsocket

Blackstone River

Chepachet River

Woonasquatucket River

Pawtucket

▲ Jerimoth Hill   812 ft.

CONNECTICUT

Scituate Reservoir

PROVIDENCE ★

Cranston

Pautuxet River

Warwick

Narragansett Bay

Prudence Island

Conanicut Island

Aquidneck Island (Rhode Island)

Bristol

Little Compton

Newport

Narragansett

Queen River

Wood River

Worden Pond

Watchaug Pond

Pawcatuck River

Atlantic Ocean

Block Island

State tree: The red maple always has some red, no matter what the season—red flowers, red leaf stalks, and of course brilliant scarlet leaves in autumn.

State flower: Violet

Endangered species: Loggerhead sea turtles are accidentally caught in shrimp nets while hunting for mollusks, horseshoe crabs, and sponges.

"The Cradle of American Industry" began at the "place of rushing water" in 1793, when Samuel Slater built a water-powered cotton spinning machine from memory of ones he used in Great Britain.

Roger Williams (1603-1683) was befriended by the Massosoit and bought land in 1636 to settle Providence, where religious and political freedom were prized.

Jewelry and silverware are Rhode Island's leading products.

In 1954, Newport held its first jazz festival—now world famous.

Sailboat races and Navy training are big activities along the Atlantic Coast.

State bird: Rhode Island Red

The Rhode Island Red chicken breed was developed in 1854. Soon the quality and quantity of eggs and the taste made chicken farming a big industry.

Rhode Island
Ocean State

13th state • Statehood: May 29, 1790 • Population: 1,048,319 • Area: 1,545 square miles

"Peachoid" is a giant water tank in Gaffney built to honor the state's fine peach crops.

Excellent banjo and fiddle players come from the Blue Ridge Mountains.

State bird: Carolina wren

Hides in moist thickets and sings "teakettle" with great energy.

State flower: Carolina Yellow jessamine grows in every corner of the state.

Sassafras Mt. 3,560 ft.
Blue Ridge Mountains
Lake Keowee
Gaffney
Spartanburg
Greenville
Rock Hill
NORTH CAROLINA

State tree: Palmetto. In 1776, its logs were used to build a small fort to defeat a British fleet in Charleston Harbor.

Hartwell Lake
Saluda River
Broad River
Wateree River
Lynches River
Pee Dee River
COLUMBIA
Lake Murray
Congaree River
Sumter
Lake Marion
Myrtle Beach

Pirates terrorized the Carolina coast in 1717-1718.

GEORGIA
Savannah River
Edisto River
Cowbahee River
Lake Moultrie
North Charleston
Santee River
Charleston
Edisto Island
Atlantic Ocean

South Carolina fought 137 battles in the Revolutionary War. Some daring militia hid in swamps to defeat the British in surprise raids.

A native of SC, the mantis hunts for other insects to eat.

Hilton Head Island

Beautiful beaches and good fishing attract millions to South Carolina.

Endangered species: The wood stork is the only true stork in the U.S.A. It fishes by touch in flooded, shallow wetlands, holding its beak open to snap up fish that swim by.

State insect: Carolina mantis

South Carolina
Palmetto State

8th state • Statehood: May 23, 1788 • Population: 4,012,012 • Area: 32,008 square miles

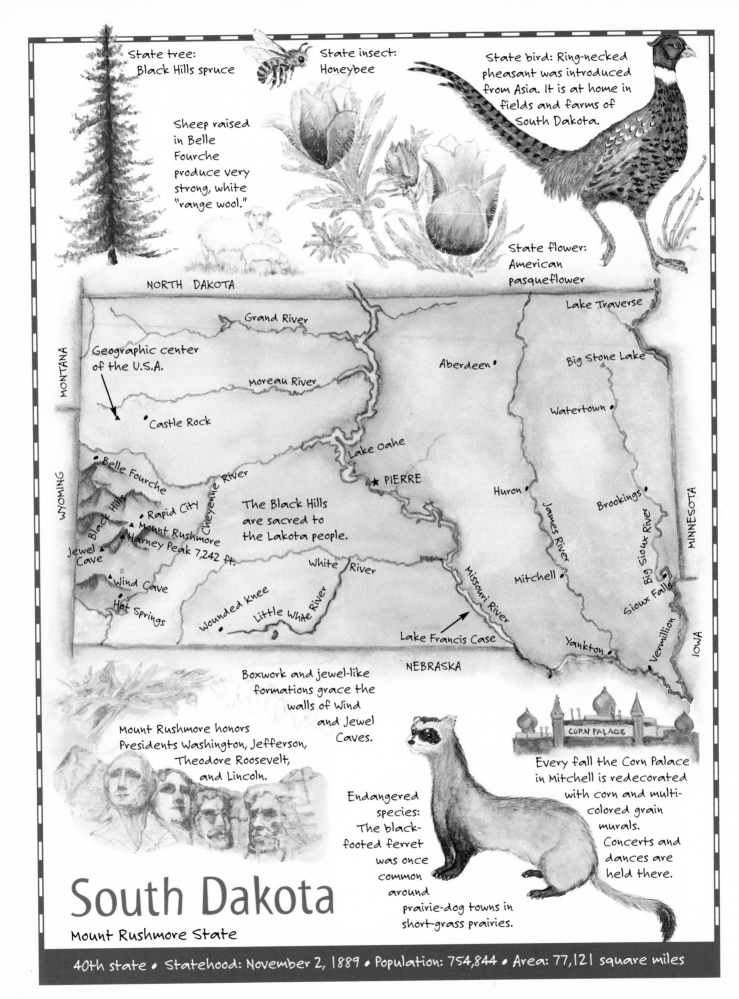

State tree: Black Hills spruce

State insect: Honeybee

State bird: Ring-necked pheasant was introduced from Asia. It is at home in fields and farms of South Dakota.

Sheep raised in Belle Fourche produce very strong, white "range wool."

State flower: American pasqueflower

NORTH DAKOTA

Grand River

Geographic center of the U.S.A.

Moreau River

MONTANA

Castle Rock

Aberdeen

Lake Traverse

Big Stone Lake

Watertown

Lake Oahe

★ PIERRE

Belle Fourche

Cheyenne River

The Black Hills are sacred to the Lakota people.

Huron

Brookings

James River

WYOMING

Rapid City

Black Hills

Mount Rushmore

Harney Peak 7,242 ft.

Jewel Cave

Wind Cave

White River

Mitchell

Big Sioux River

MINNESOTA

Hot Springs

Wounded Knee

Little White River

Missouri River

Lake Francis Case

Sioux Falls

Vermillion

Yankton

IOWA

NEBRASKA

Boxwork and jewel-like formations grace the walls of Wind and Jewel Caves.

CORN PALACE

Mount Rushmore honors Presidents Washington, Jefferson, Theodore Roosevelt, and Lincoln.

Endangered species: The black-footed ferret was once common around prairie-dog towns in short-grass prairies.

Every fall the Corn Palace in Mitchell is redecorated with corn and multi-colored grain murals. Concerts and dances are held there.

South Dakota

Mount Rushmore State

40th state • Statehood: November 2, 1889 • Population: 754,844 • Area: 77,121 square miles

State tree: Tulip poplar

State bird: The mockingbird is a talented and varied singer in a state famous for different kinds of music: bluegrass, rock 'n' roll, blues, and country.

Davy Crockett was a frontiersman and a gifted storyteller. His motto was "Be always sure you're right—then go ahead."

(1786-1836)

In December 1811, a violent earthquake made the Mississippi River change course, and a giant wave created Reelfoot Lake.

State insects: Firefly and ladybug

KENTUCKY

VIRGINIA

MISSOURI

Reelfoot Lake

Cumberland River

Cumberland Mts.

Appalachian Mts.

ARKANSAS

Mississippi River

Tennessee River

NASHVILLE

Cumberland Plateau

Oak Ridge

Knoxville

Clingmans Dome 6,643 ft.

Great Smoky Mountains

Tennessee River

Shelbyville

NORTH CAROLINA

Memphis

MISSISSIPPI

ALABAMA

Chattanooga

GEORGIA

Endangered species: Spruce-fir moss spider. This tiny tarantula (1/10") lives only on moss-covered boulders in old-growth forests.

The Sunsphere Tower at Knoxville's 1982 World's Fair symbolized the fair's theme, "Energy Turns the World."

State flower: Iris

State wildflower: The passionflower was the original state flower. In 1933, it was changed to the state wildflower.

Tennessee walking horses are raised near Shelbyville and prized for their smooth gait.

Tennessee

Volunteer State

16th state • Statehood: June 1, 1796 • Population: 5,689,283 • Area: 42,146 square miles

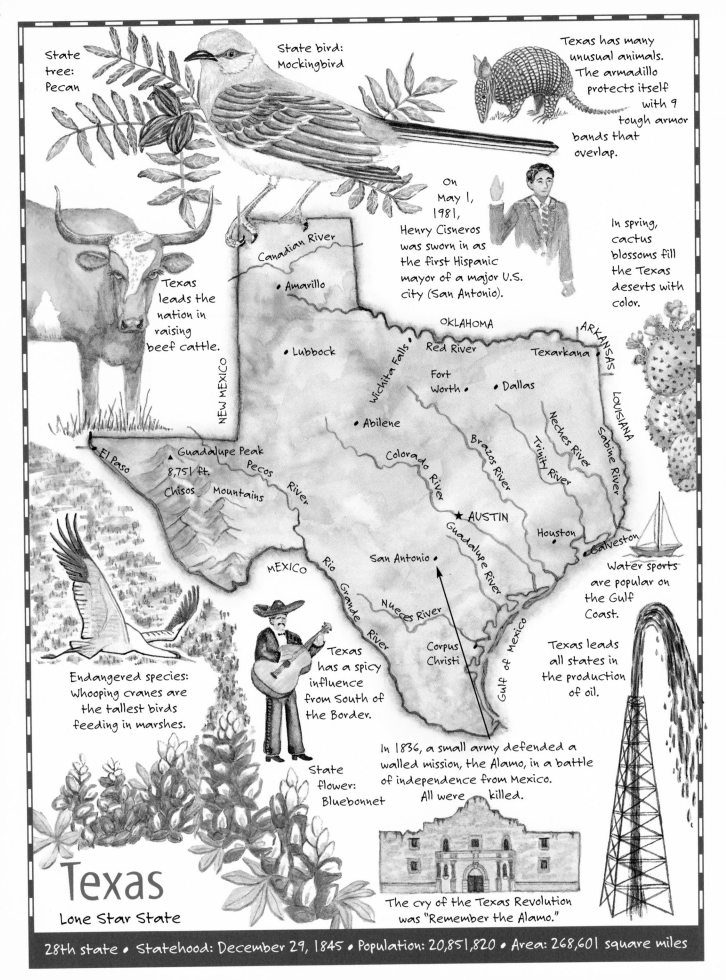

State tree: Pecan

State bird: Mockingbird

Texas has many unusual animals. The armadillo protects itself with 9 tough armor bands that overlap.

On May 1, 1981, Henry Cisneros was sworn in as the first Hispanic mayor of a major U.S. city (San Antonio).

In spring, cactus blossoms fill the Texas deserts with color.

Texas leads the nation in raising beef cattle.

OKLAHOMA

ARKANSAS

LOUISIANA

NEW MEXICO

Canadian River

• Amarillo

• Lubbock

Red River

Wichita Falls •

Texarkana

Fort Worth •

• Dallas

• Abilene

Neches River

Trinity River

Sabine River

El Paso

Guadalupe Peak 8,751 ft.

Pecos River

Colorado River

Brazos River

Chisos Mountains

★ AUSTIN

Guadalupe River

Houston

Galveston

Water sports are popular on the Gulf Coast.

MEXICO

Rio Grande River

San Antonio •

Nueces River

Gulf of Mexico

Corpus Christi

Texas leads all states in the production of oil.

Endangered species: Whooping cranes are the tallest birds feeding in marshes.

Texas has a spicy influence from South of the Border.

State flower: Bluebonnet

In 1836, a small army defended a walled mission, the Alamo, in a battle of independence from Mexico. All were killed.

Texas

Lone Star State

The cry of the Texas Revolution was "Remember the Alamo."

28th state • Statehood: December 29, 1845 • Population: 20,851,820 • Area: 268,601 square miles

State bird: Sea gulls live on the shores of the Great Salt Lake.

The world's first transcontinental railroad joined East to West in Promontory in 1869.

State tree: Blue spruce

Hard-packed salt flats are often where car speed records are set.

The Great Salt Lake is saltier than any ocean, so it's easy to float on it.

Endangered species: The Utah prairie dogs live in large colonies called dog towns.

The Navajo weave rugs, raise sheep, and make turquoise and silver jewelry.

Brigham Young led the Mormons from Missouri in search of religious freedom. On July 24, 1847, he first saw the Salt Lake Valley and said, "This is the place."

Later, over 4,000 settlers pulled handcarts to Utah.

State insect: Honeybee

Southern Utah has many national parks with spectacular arches, spires, and canyons.

"Big Indian" in Monument Valley

Rainbow Bridge National Monument

State flower: Sego lily

Utah
Beehive State

IDAHO

WYOMING

NEVADA

COLORADO

ARIZONA

NEW MEXICO

Promontory

Wasatch Range

Great Salt Lake

Ogden

Bountiful

SALT LAKE CITY

Great Salt Lake Desert

Basin

Great

Utah Lake

Provo

Fairview

Kings Peak, 13,528 ft.

Uinta Mountains

Green River

Arches National Park

Colorado Plateau

Dirty Devil River

Canyonlands National Park

Colorado River

Sevier River

Capitol Reef National Park

Bryce Canyon National Park

Escalante Desert

Rainbow Bridge

Zion National Park

Lake Powell

San Juan River

Monument Valley

4 Corners

Bonneville Speedway

45th state • Statehood: January 4, 1896 • Population: 2,233,169 • Area: 84,904 square miles

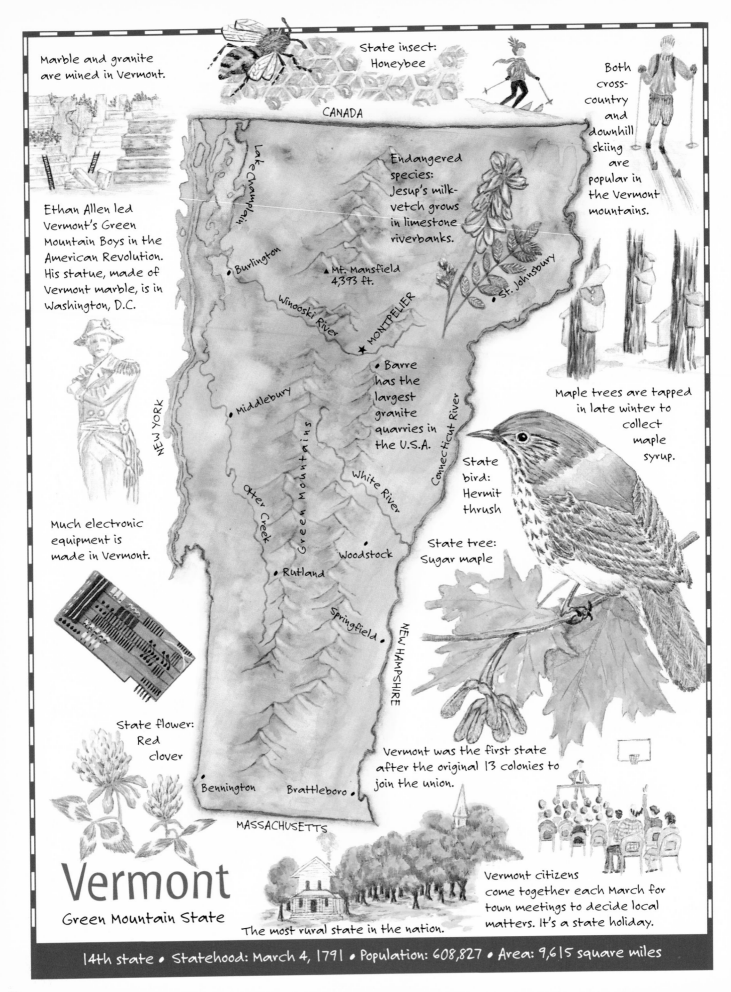

Marble and granite are mined in Vermont.

State insect: Honeybee

Both cross-country and downhill skiing are popular in the Vermont mountains.

CANADA

Ethan Allen led Vermont's Green Mountain Boys in the American Revolution. His statue, made of Vermont marble, is in Washington, D.C.

Endangered species: Jesup's milk-vetch grows in limestone riverbanks.

Lake Champlain

• Burlington

▲ Mt. Mansfield 4,393 ft.

Winooski River

MONTPELIER ★

• St. Johnsbury

NEW YORK

• Middlebury

• Barre has the largest granite quarries in the U.S.A.

Connecticut River

White River

Maple trees are tapped in late winter to collect maple syrup.

State bird: Hermit thrush

Much electronic equipment is made in Vermont.

Green Mountains

Otter Creek

Woodstock

State tree: Sugar maple

• Rutland

Springfield •

NEW HAMPSHIRE

State flower: Red clover

Vermont was the first state after the original 13 colonies to join the union.

• Bennington

Brattleboro •

MASSACHUSETTS

Vermont

Green Mountain State

The most rural state in the nation.

Vermont citizens come together each March for town meetings to decide local matters. It's a state holiday.

14th state • Statehood: March 4, 1791 • Population: 608,827 • Area: 9,615 square miles

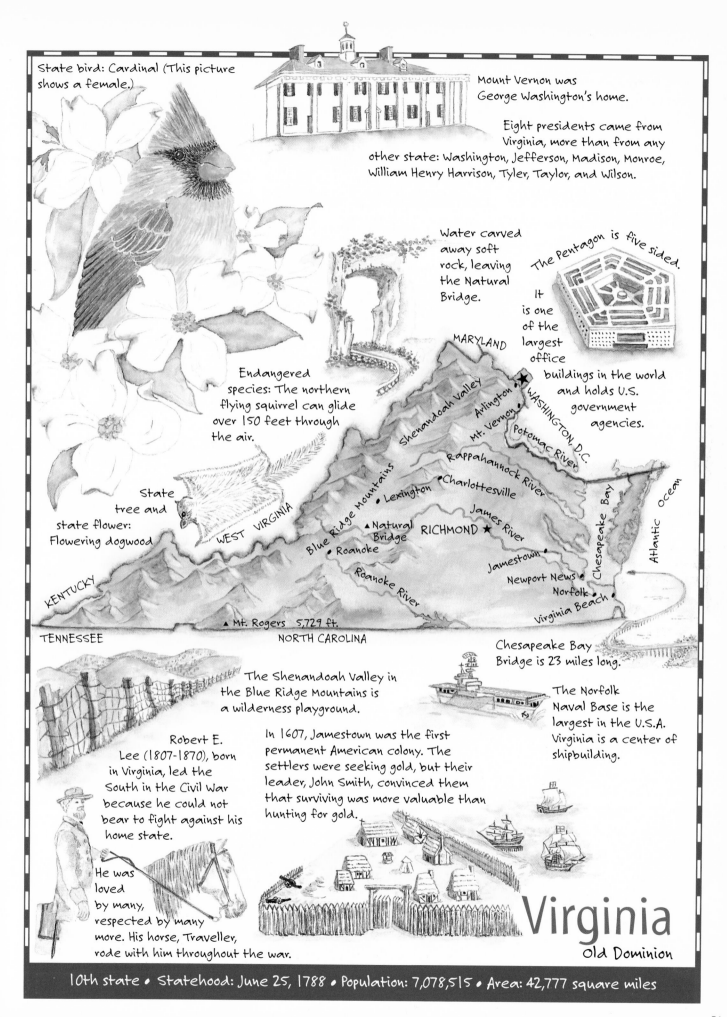

State bird: Cardinal (This picture shows a female.)

Mount Vernon was George Washington's home.

Eight presidents came from Virginia, more than from any other state: Washington, Jefferson, Madison, Monroe, William Henry Harrison, Tyler, Taylor, and Wilson.

Water carved away soft rock, leaving the Natural Bridge.

The Pentagon is five sided. It is one of the largest office buildings in the world and holds U.S. government agencies.

Endangered species: The northern flying squirrel can glide over 150 feet through the air.

State tree and state flower: Flowering dogwood

MARYLAND

Shenandoah Valley
Arlington
WASHINGTON, D.C.
Mt. Vernon
Potomac River
Rappahannock River
Charlottesville
Lexington
James River
RICHMOND
Natural Bridge
Blue Ridge Mountains
Roanoke
Jamestown
Newport News
Norfolk
Virginia Beach
Roanoke River
Chesapeake Bay
Atlantic Ocean

WEST VIRGINIA

KENTUCKY

TENNESSEE

▲ Mt. Rogers 5,729 ft.

NORTH CAROLINA

The Shenandoah Valley in the Blue Ridge Mountains is a wilderness playground.

Chesapeake Bay Bridge is 23 miles long.

The Norfolk Naval Base is the largest in the U.S.A. Virginia is a center of shipbuilding.

Robert E. Lee (1807-1870), born in Virginia, led the South in the Civil War because he could not bear to fight against his home state.

He was loved by many, respected by many more. His horse, Traveller, rode with him throughout the war.

In 1607, Jamestown was the first permanent American colony. The settlers were seeking gold, but their leader, John Smith, convinced them that surviving was more valuable than hunting for gold.

Virginia
Old Dominion

10th state • Statehood: June 25, 1788 • Population: 7,078,515 • Area: 42,777 square miles

Washington grows more apples than anywhere else in the U.S.A.

Tacoma has the world's tallest totem pole, 105 feet high. Many Pacific Northwest tribes have family or clan emblems on their poles.

Endangered species: Olive ridley sea turtles mate in the Pacific Ocean.

State flower: Coast rhododendron loves the rain-forest climate of western Washington.

CANADA

San Juan Islands

Strait of Juan de Fuca

Bellingham

Skagit River

Cascade Mountains

Wenatchee River

Lake Chelan

Okanogan River

Rocky Mountains

Pend Oreille River

IDAHO

Puget Sound

Olympic Mountains

Grand Coulee Dam

Spokane River

Spokane

Seattle

Pacific Ocean

Tacoma

Wenatchee

Columbia River

Columbia Plateau

★OLYMPIA

Centralia

Mt. Rainer 14,410 ft.

Yakima

Yakima River

Snake River

Walla Walla

Mt. St. Helens erupted May 18, 1980, spitting ashes around the world.

Columbia River

OREGON

Vancouver

The Space Needle, a tower in Seattle, is 607 feet high. An elevator takes people to see the view from the top.

State tree: Western hemlock and other evergreens cover half the state.

Sockeye and chinook salmon are born in freshwater rivers, swim to the ocean, and return to their birthplace to spawn.

The only state named after a president

State bird: Goldfinch. These "wild canaries" are found coast to coast.

Washington

Evergreen State

42nd state • Statehood: November 11, 1889 • Population: 5,894,121 • Area: 71,302 square miles

State bird: Cardinal

Folk music is very popular, and many people still make their own instruments.

State tree: Sugar maple

Homemade quilts, clothes, and furniture are traditional.

West Virginia is famous for its pottery, glassware, and marbles.

PENNSYLVANIA

Weirton

Wheeling

OHIO

Ohio River

Parkersburg

Morgantown

Fairmont

Cheat River

MARYLAND

Tygart Lake

Potomac River

Appalachian Mountains

Allegheny Mountains

Harpers Ferry

Shenandoah River

Kanawha River

Elk River

Sutton Lake

Tygart Valley River

Cheat Mountains

Spruce Knob 4,863 ft.

Endangered species: The Cheat Mountain salamander lives in moist woodlands,

CHARLESTON

Huntington

Guyandotte River

Tug Fork River

KENTUCKY

New River

Beckley

Summerville Lake

Greenbrier River

Big Bend Tunnel

Bluestone River

Lewisburg

VIRGINIA

breathing through its skin—it has no lungs.

State flower: The rhododendron grows on moist mountain slopes all over West Virginia.

In the 1870s, Big Bend Tunnel worker John Henry competed with a steam-powered drill and proved he could work faster than a machine.

Almost 2,000 miles of white water provide the best canoeing, kayaking, and rafting east of the Mississippi.

West Virginia

Mountain State

35th state • Statehood: June 20, 1863 • Population: 1,808,344 • Area: 24,231 square miles

Wisconsin has beautiful, deep forests. It produces more paper than any other state.

State bird: Robin

State tree: Sugar maples provide shade and syrup.

Every February, Hayward holds the largest cross-country race in the U.S.A.

Lake Superior
Superior
Hayward
Iron Belt
Presque Isle
MICHIGAN
St. Croix River
MINNESOTA
Eagle River
Timms Hill 1,952 ft.
Wolf River
Chippewa River
Eau Claire
Wausau
Black River
Stevens Point
Green Bay
State insect: Honeybee
Mississippi River
La Crosse
Scenic river gorge called the Wisconsin Dells
Green Bay
Appleton
Lake Winnebago
Oshkosh
Sheboygan
Fond du Lac
Lake Michigan
State flower: Wood violet
Wisconsin River
Watertown
Milwaukee
Iowa
MADISON ★
Racine
Kenosha
Beloit
ILLINOIS

Endangered species: The dwarf lake iris likes sandy soil near the shores of Lake Michigan.

Early lead miners lived in caves they dug into hillsides, much like badgers build their homes.

Wisconsin
Badger State

"America's Dairyland" leads the nation in milk and cheese production.

In 1856, Watertown held the first kindergarten class in the U.S.A.

ORANGE
BLUE

30th state • Statehood: May 29, 1848 • Population: 5,363,675 • Area: 65,499 square miles

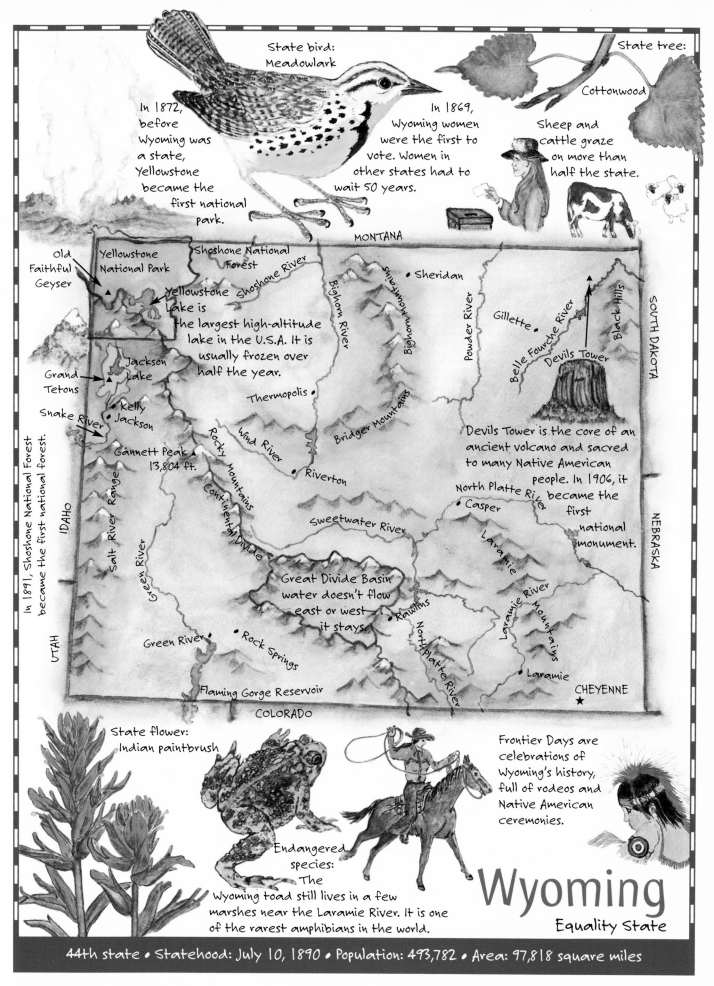

State bird: Meadowlark

State tree: Cottonwood

In 1872, before Wyoming was a state, Yellowstone became the first national park.

In 1869, Wyoming women were the first to vote. Women in other states had to wait 50 years.

Sheep and cattle graze on more than half the state.

MONTANA

Old Faithful Geyser

Yellowstone National Park

Shoshone National Forest

Shoshone River

• Sheridan

Bighorn River

Shivishne Mountains

Bighorn Mountains

Powder River

Gillette •

Belle Fourche River

Black Hills

Devils Tower

SOUTH DAKOTA

Yellowstone Lake is the largest high-altitude lake in the U.S.A. It is usually frozen over half the year.

Grand Tetons

Jackson Lake

Snake River

• Kelly
• Jackson

In 1891, Shoshone National Forest became the first national forest.

Gannett Peak 13,804 ft.

Rocky Mountains

Wind River

Thermopolis •

Bridger Mountains

• Riverton

Salt River Range

Green River

Continental Divide

Sweetwater River

North Platte River

• Casper

Devils Tower is the core of an ancient volcano and sacred to many Native American people. In 1906, it became the first national monument.

IDAHO

UTAH

Great Divide Basin water doesn't flow east or west— it stays.

• Rawlins

Green River •

• Rock Springs

North Platte River

Laramie River

Laramie Mountains

• Laramie

NEBRASKA

Flaming Gorge Reservoir

CHEYENNE ★

COLORADO

State flower: Indian paintbrush

Endangered species: The Wyoming toad still lives in a few marshes near the Laramie River. It is one of the rarest amphibians in the world.

Frontier Days are celebrations of Wyoming's history, full of rodeos and Native American ceremonies.

Wyoming
Equality State

44th state • Statehood: July 10, 1890 • Population: 493,782 • Area: 97,818 square miles

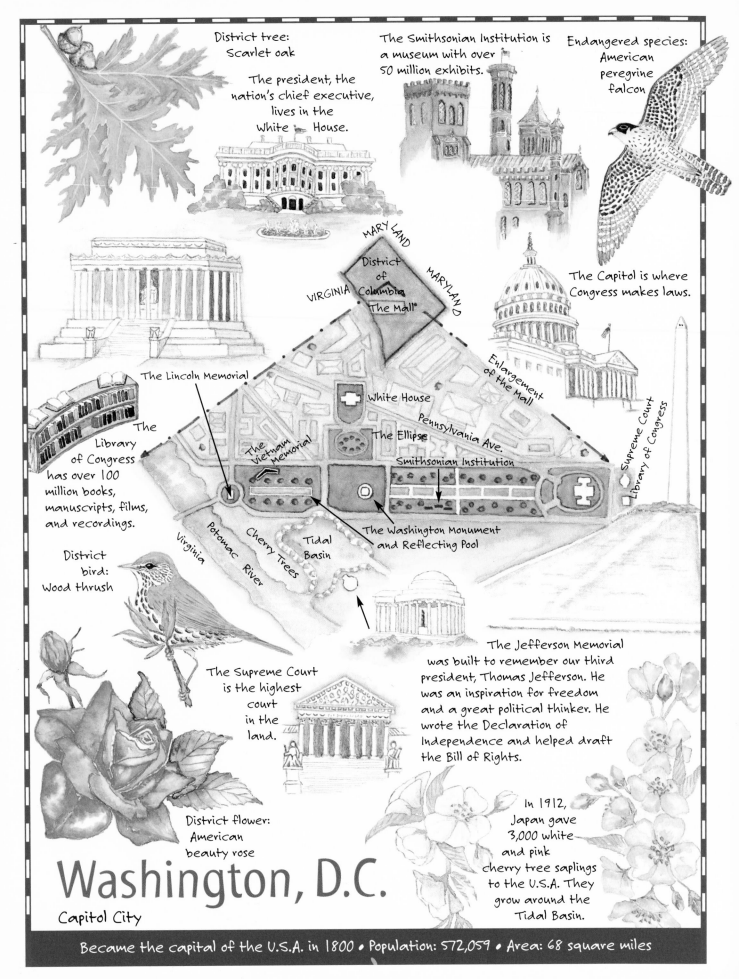

District tree: Scarlet oak

The Smithsonian Institution is a museum with over 50 million exhibits.

Endangered species: American peregrine falcon

The president, the nation's chief executive, lives in the White House.

The Capitol is where Congress makes laws.

MARYLAND

MARYLAND

VIRGINIA

District of Columbia

The Mall

Enlargement of the Mall

The Lincoln Memorial

White House

Pennsylvania Ave.

The Library of Congress has over 100 million books, manuscripts, films, and recordings.

The Vietnam Memorial

The Ellipse

Smithsonian Institution

Supreme Court

Library of Congress

District bird: Wood thrush

Virginia

Potomac River

Cherry Trees

Tidal Basin

The Washington Monument and Reflecting Pool

The Supreme Court is the highest court in the land.

The Jefferson Memorial was built to remember our third president, Thomas Jefferson. He was an inspiration for freedom and a great political thinker. He wrote the Declaration of Independence and helped draft the Bill of Rights.

District flower: American beauty rose

In 1912, Japan gave 3,000 white and pink cherry tree saplings to the U.S.A. They grow around the Tidal Basin.

Washington, D.C.

Capitol City

Became the capital of the U.S.A. in 1800 • Population: 572,059 • Area: 68 square miles

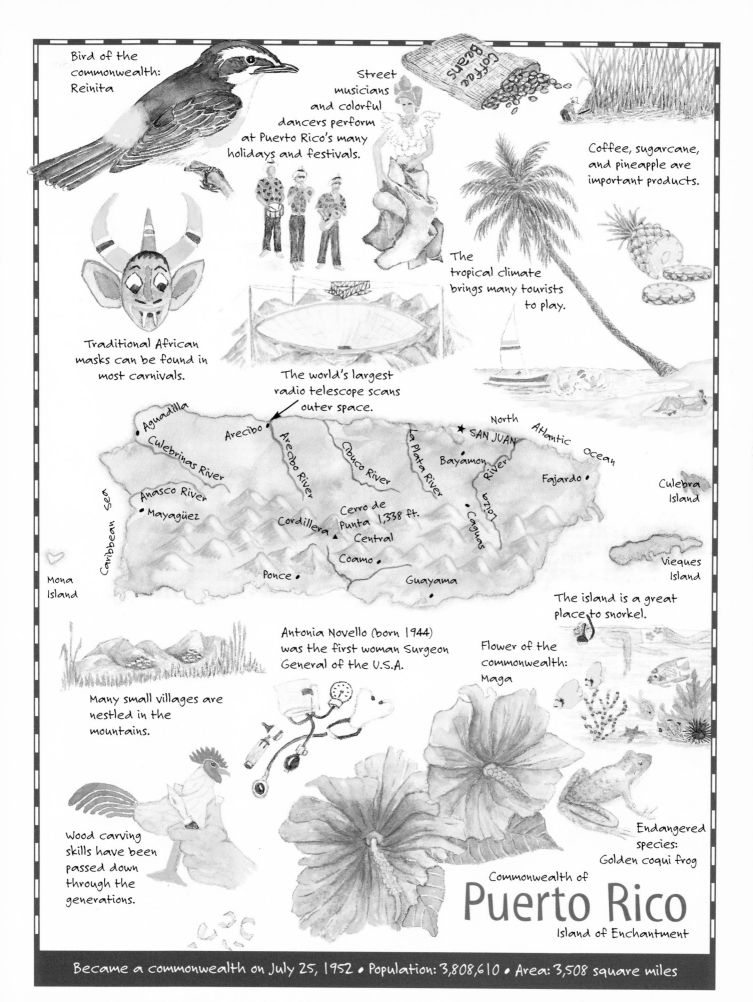

Bird of the commonwealth: Reinita

Street musicians and colorful dancers perform at Puerto Rico's many holidays and festivals.

Coffee, sugarcane, and pineapple are important products.

Traditional African masks can be found in most carnivals.

The world's largest radio telescope scans outer space.

The tropical climate brings many tourists to play.

North Atlantic Ocean

Aguadilla
Arecibo
Culebrinas River
Arecibo River
Cibuco River
La Plata River
SAN JUAN
Bayamon
River
Fajardo
Culebra Island
Anasco River
Mayagüez
Cordillera
Cerro de Punta 1,338 ft.
Central
Caguas
Loiza
Caribbean Sea
Coamo
Vieques Island
Ponce
Guayama
Mona Island

The island is a great place to snorkel.

Many small villages are nestled in the mountains.

Antonia Novello (born 1944) was the first woman Surgeon General of the U.S.A.

Flower of the commonwealth: Maga

Wood carving skills have been passed down through the generations.

Endangered species: Golden coqui frog

Commonwealth of
Puerto Rico
Island of Enchantment

Became a commonwealth on July 25, 1952 • Population: 3,808,610 • Area: 3,508 square miles

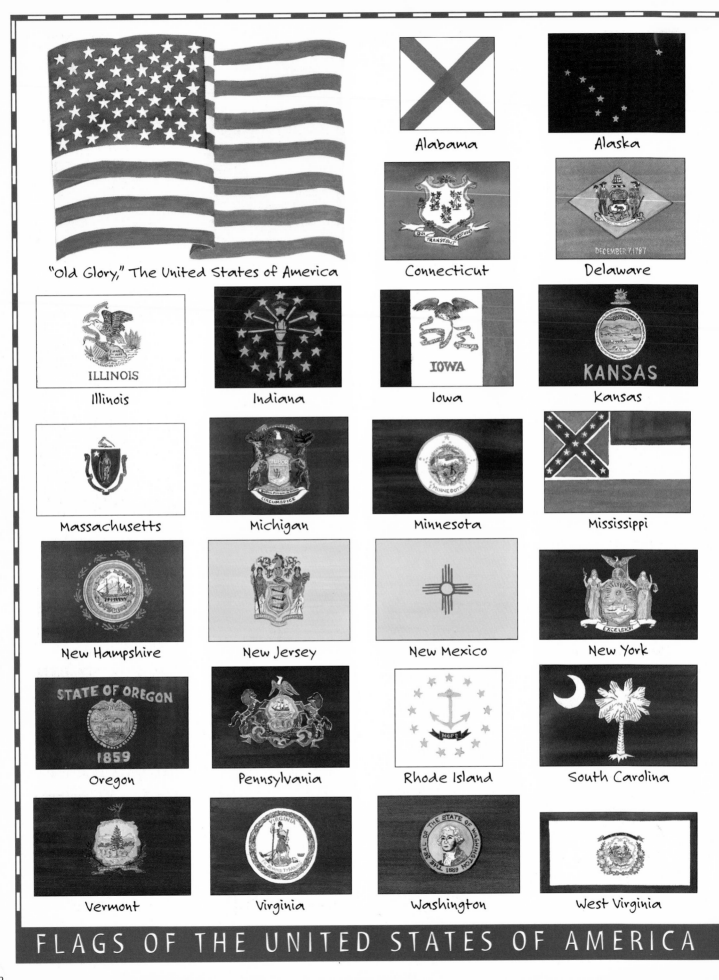

"Old Glory," The United States of America

Alabama

Alaska

Connecticut

Delaware

Illinois

Indiana

Iowa

Kansas

Massachusetts

Michigan

Minnesota

Mississippi

New Hampshire

New Jersey

New Mexico

New York

Oregon

Pennsylvania

Rhode Island

South Carolina

Vermont

Virginia

Washington

West Virginia

FLAGS OF THE UNITED STATES OF AMERICA

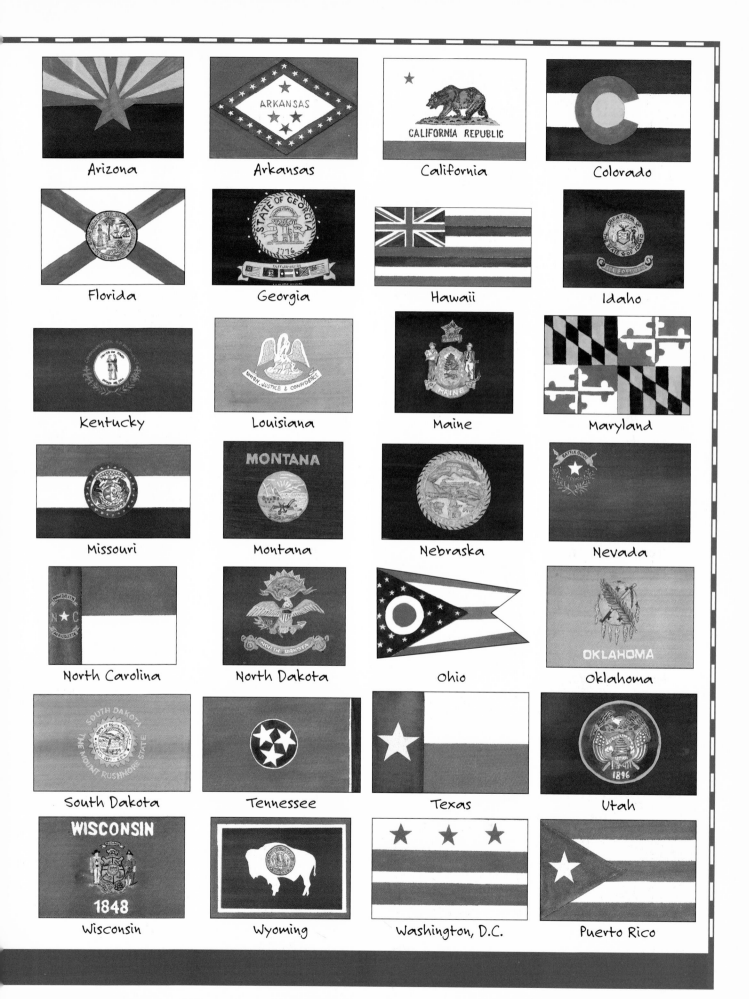

Arizona

Arkansas

California

Colorado

Florida

Georgia

Hawaii

Idaho

Kentucky

Louisiana

Maine

Maryland

Missouri

Montana

Nebraska

Nevada

North Carolina

North Dakota

Ohio

Oklahoma

South Dakota

Tennessee

Texas

Utah

Wisconsin

Wyoming

Washington, D.C.

Puerto Rico

INDEX

Henry, John, 53
Rogers, Will, 41
Twain, Mark, 30
Webster, Noah, 12

Endangered Species

American hart's-tongue fern, 37
American peregrine falcon, 56
black-capped vireo, 21
black-footed ferret, 46
California condor, 10
Carolina parakeet (extinct), 5
Cheat Mountain
    salamander, 53
Delmarva Peninsula fox
    squirrel, 13
desert tortoise, 33
dwarf lake iris, 54
eastern indigo snake, 15
Eskimo curlew, 39
Florida manatee, 14
Furbish lousewort, 24
golden coqui frog, 57
gopher tortoise, 29
gray wolf, 28
greenback cutthroat trout, 11
Hawaiian monk seal, 16
hawksbill sea turtle, 12
Hine's emerald dragonfly, 18
humpback whale, 7
Indiana bat, 19
Iowa Pleistocene snail, 20
Jessup's milkvetch, 50
Kentucky cave shrimp, 22
Kirkland's warbler, 27
Kramer blue butterfly, 34
lakeside daisy, 40
loggerhead sea turtle, 44
Louisiana black bear, 23
Maryland darter, 25
Missouri bladderpod, 30

New Mexican ridgenose
    rattlesnake, 36
northern flying squirrel, 51
northern riffle shell mussel, 43
northern spotted owl, 42
olive ridley sea turtle, 52
Ozark cavefish, 9
piping plover, 41
Plymouth red-bellied turtle, 26
Red Hills salamander, 6
red wolf, 38
roseate tern, 35
Sandborn's lesser long-nosed
    bat, 8
spruce-fir moss spider, 47
Utah prairie dog, 49
whooping crane, 48
woodland caribou, 17
wood stork, 45
Wyoming toad, 55

Geographic Attractions

Badlands, 39
Boundary Waters Canoe Area,
    28
Cape Cod, 26
caves, 6, 9, 17, 18, 19, 22,
    36, 46
Chesapeake Bay, 25
Death Valley, 4, 10
dells, 54
Dinosaur National Monument,
    11
Everglades, 14
Florida Keys, 14
Glacier National Park, 31
Grand Canyon, 8
Grand Tetons, 55
Great Salt Lake, 49
Jersey shore, 35
Lake Mead, 33
Las Vegas, 33

Monument Valley, 49
Niagara Falls, 37
Old Man of the Mountains, 34
Outer Banks, 38
Painted Desert, 8
Petrified Forest, 8
Rainbow Bridge, 49
Sequoia National Park, 10
Shenandoah Valley, 51
Wye Oak Tree, 25
Yellowstone National Park,
    31, 55
Yosemite National Park, 10

Holidays

Arbor Day, 32
Frontier Days, 55
Mardi Gras, 23
Vermont town meetings, 50

Landmarks

Arctic Circle, 7
Continental Divide, 4, 11, 17,
    31, 36, 55
deepest canyon in U.S., 42
deepest lake in U.S., 42
easternmost point in U.S.,
    5, 24
Four Corners, 8, 11, 36, 49
geographic center of U.S., 21, 46
Great Lakes, 5, 21, 27
highest natural lake, 55
highest peak in U.S., 4, 7
hottest temperature in U.S., 10
largest freshwater lake in the
    world, 5, 28
longest canal in the world, 5
longest undefended border in
    the world, 4
lowest dry land in U.S., 4, 10
Mason Dixon Line, 25

Sports

baseball, 15, 19, 37

basketball, 26, 27

bicycling, 33

car racing, 19, 49

fishing, 28, 45

horse racing, 22

hot air balloons, 36

Iditarod, 7

marathon, 26

National Baseball Hall of Fame, 37

Olympics, 37

Pro Football Hall of Fame, 40

rodeos, 31, 55

skiing, 11, 17, 50, 54

snorkeling, 57

snowshoeing, 28

Superdome, 23

surfing, 16

volleyball, 26

water sports, 24, 27, 28, 44, 45, 48, 53

State Birds

bald eagle (national bird), 4

Baltimore oriole, 25

black-capped chickadee, 24, 25, 26

bluebird, 30, 37

blue hen chicken, 13

brown pelican, 23

brown thrasher, 15

cactus wren, 8

California valley quail, 10

cardinal, 18, 19, 22, 38, 40, 51, 53

Carolina wren, 45

common loon, 28

goldfinch, 20, 35, 52

hermit thrush, 50

lark bunting, 11

meadowlark, 21, 31, 32, 39, 42, 55

mockingbird, 9, 14, 29, 47, 48

mountain bluebird, 17, 33

nene, 16

purple finch, 34

reinita, 57

Rhode Island Red, 44

ring-necked pheasant, 46

roadrunner, 36

robin, 12, 27, 54

ruffed grouse, 43

scissor-tailed flycatcher, 41

sea gull, 49

willow ptarmigan, 7

wood thrush, 56

yellow-shafted flicker, 6

State Flowers

American beauty rose (national flower), 5, 56

apple blossom, 9, 27

bitterroot, 31

black-eyed Susan, 25

bluebonnet, 48

camellia, 6

Carolina yellow jessamine, 45

Cherokee rose, 15

coastal rhododendron, 52

flowering dogwood, 38, 51

forget-me-not, 7

golden poppy, 10

goldenrod, 22, 32

hawthorn, 30

hibiscus, 16

Indian paintbrush, 55

iris, 47

maga, 57

magnolia, 23, 29

mayflower, 26

mistletoe, 41

mountain laurel, 12, 43

orange blossom, 14

Oregon grape, 42

pasqueflower, 46

peach blossom, 13

peony, 19

purple lilac, 34

red clover, 50

rhododendron, 53

Rocky Mountain columbine, 11

rose, 37

sagebrush, 33

saguaro cactus blossom, 8

scarlet carnation, 40

sego lily, 49

showy lady slipper, 28

sunflower, 21

syringa, 17

violet, 18, 35, 44

white pine cone and tassel, 24

wild prairie rose, 39

wild rose, 20

wood violet, 54

yucca, 36

State Insects

Baltimore checkerspot, 25

California dogface, 10

Carolina mantis, 45

Colorado hairstreak, 11

firefly, 43, 47

giant swallowtail, 14

honeybee, 9, 15, 21, 23, 24, 29, 30, 32, 35, 38, 46, 49, 50, 54

ladybug, 13, 20, 26, 34, 37, 40, 47

monarch, 6, 17, 18

praying mantis, 12

spicebush swallowtail, 29

tarantula hawk wasp, 36

State Trees

American elm, 39